REINCARNATION
A CHRISTIAN APPRAISAL

MARK
ALBRECHT

InterVarsity Press
Downers Grove
Illinois 60515

InterVarsity Press is the book-publishing division of Inter-Varsity Christian Fellowship, a student movement active on campus at hundreds of universities, colleges and schools of nursing. For information about local and regional activities, write IVCF, 233 Langdon St., Madison, WI 53703.

Distributed in Canada through InterVarsity Press, 1875 Leslie St., Unit 10, Don Mills, Ontario M3B 2M5, Canada.

Bible quotations are from the Revised Standard Version, copyrighted 1946, 1952, © 1971, 1973, by the Division of Christian Education, National Council of the Churches of Christ in the USA, and used by permission.

Cover illustration: Jerry Tiritilli

ISBN 0-87784-378-3

Printed in the United States of America

Library of Congress Cataloging in Publication Data

Albrecht, Mark, 1947-
    Reincarnation, a Christian appraisal.

    Includes bibliographical references.
    1.   Christianity and reincarnation.
2. Reincarnation–Controversial literature.
I. Title.
BR115.R4A4   1982   236   82-16228
ISBN 0-87784-378-3

17	16	15	14	13	12	11	10	9	8	7	6	5	4	3	2	1
95	94	93	92	91	90	89	88	87	86	85	84	83	82			

Preface

When I first began to do research on reincarnation, it was not with the intention of writing a book; in fact, I really didn't want to write a book at all. I've always thought that there are far too many of them gathering dust in the bookstores and libraries of the world, and I didn't particularly want to contribute to the glut. However, I came to realize that there is a deep need for a book that asks some probing questions about reincarnation. Feeling thus compelled, I set myself to the task.

As it happened, I was working for the Spiritual Counterfeits Project in Berkeley, California, an apologetics ministry that deals primarily with new religious movements and Eastern philosophy. One of my assignments was to write a fifteen-page survey of reincarnation. As I began the research, I discovered that much has been written about reincarnation, but about ninety-five per cent of it is proreincarnation; few intelligently skeptical writings on the subject are to be found. This seemed a bit strange since the United States is at least *culturally* a Christian country. I did not expect to encounter such uncritical enthusiasm for an alien teaching. Moreover, among the many volumes of theology, philosophy of religion and comparative religion, I found no adequate critical response to the doctrine of reincarnation. Contemporary Christian appraisals of the issue have generally fallen into two predictable categories: (1) the "standard" approach, which attacks reincarnation as unbiblical and offensive, and therefore wrong, but which is noticeably lacking in explanations as to why it is wrong; and (2) the perennial attempt to syncretize or blend reincarnation with historical orthodox Christianity. Neither of these responses has been particularly useful or fruitful.

This lack of a coherent critique seemed even stranger when I realized the importance and impact of the teaching. Reincarnation is virtually a "given"—a presupposition of life—in most of the Orient, almost like gravity; and it is picking up huge blocks of support in the Western world. The 1982 Gallup Poll claims that twenty-three per cent of the U.S. population believe in some variety of this theory.[1] Worldwide, belief in some type of reincarnation stands at about fifty per cent. Why theologians and Christian thinkers have neglected a topic as important as this I cannot say; even seventeen per cent of those who "regularly attend church" allegedly believe in reincarnation.[2] Thus my interest was stirred, and the fifteen-page paper grew to many times its original length.

Although it has been a fascinating excursion to work on this subject, it has been stretching and at times even a little scary, since it brought me face to face with the ultimate concerns of human existence. Things like death: what happens after we die? Concerns like God and evil, justice and judgment, inequality and suffering, and the problem of conflicting world views. Many contrasting religions and philosophies clamor in the marketplace, claiming to have God's true program for the human race.

This paradox of conflicting truth claims made me an amateur student of comparative religion years ago, after spending some time with the Jehovah's Witnesses. I wanted not only to appreciate the various religions of the world, but to find the truth for myself. In this context, let me point out that this book is not just a history and exposition of reincarnation. As the title implies, I intend to unravel the subject from a Christian perspective, and that purpose should be clear from the outset. While I have made every effort to present the reincarnation position fairly and accurately, I will present its counterpoint from Judeo-Christian thought.

Asking hard questions by verbal poking and pommeling is really the essence of interfaith dialog; it brings out the strengths and weaknesses of any religion or philosophy. At this confusing time in history we need to learn to think critically, and nowhere is this more necessary than in religion.

Since the advent of Madame H. P. Blavatsky's Theosophy-inspired syncretism and the Hindu countermission to the West (both in the last hundred years), reincarnation philosophy has established a growing beachhead in Western society, and the influence of this pivotal teaching has increased in direct proportion to the explosion of religious pluralism that has characterized the last two decades. Thus it cannot be ignored. Whether reincarnation is a philosophy "fitting for the chatter of frogs and fishes," as St. Gregory of Nyssa thought in the fourth century, or "a most comforting explanation of reality," as Albert Schweitzer once said, is the question before us. Whatever the answer may be, it is of utmost importance for those who believe in a life after death.

I would like to thank Dr. Gordon Fee and Dr. Douglas Stuart, professors of New Testament and Old Testament respectively at Gordon-Conwell Theological Seminary, South Hamilton, Massachusetts, for their help with portions of the book. My thanks also go to Philly Roob and Betsy Joy for their fine typing and deciphering of my hieroglyphics. And finally, I would like to thank and acknowledge my parents, Walter and Leona Albrecht, who taught me at an early age to think about God. No greater thought can occupy the human mind.

1
Reincarnation East and West

ON DECEMBER 7, 1977, ELDON McCorkhill, 33, and Linda Cummings, 28, were sitting in a bar in Redlands, California, having a few drinks and chatting. The subject eventually turned to life after death, and Linda told Eldon that she was firmly convinced of the reality of reincarnation. Eldon scoffed loudly and a spirited debate ensued. They argued all the way back to McCorkhill's apartment; once there, he pulled a loaded pistol out of his drawer and handed it to her.

"If you believe in this, let's see what you'll come back as," he said. Linda took the gun, pointed it to her head and pulled the trigger.[1]

While this true story is hardly an accurate reflection of the influence of belief in reincarnation in America today, it does underscore an undeniable fact: Belief in reincarnation has been growing swiftly in the Western world. Fifty years ago the public at large regarded such beliefs as fringe lunacy or oriental occult superstition. Today nothing could be further from the truth. Reincarnation is gathering believers by the hundreds, if not thousands, each day. Stories about hypnotic "regressions" and spontaneous "recalls of former lives" are almost regular features in newspapers and magazines.

The multitude of gurus, gopis, lamas, psychics and living masters that have surfaced in the United States and Europe in the last twenty years have offered an almost endless variety of speculative metaphysical philosophies, many of which find their ideological foundations in the traditional religions of the Orient. One of the basic tenets of these religions is the ancient doctrine of reincarnation or rebirth (also called "transmigration" or "metempsychosis"): the idea that our soul or essence is in some way passed on after we die and injected into a new body at birth.

Reincarnation is no fad. It has been an essential element of Hindu and Buddhist thought since well before Christ, and it still constitutes one of the central presuppositions of the oriental world view. Statistically, the belief in and influence of reincarnation is staggering. Approximately fifty per cent of the world's population adhere to some form of this concept, and this figure may be conservative. In the West, a 1969 Gallup Poll indicated that an average of twenty to twenty-five per cent (depending on the country) of the population of the United States and Western Europe believed in reincarnation or considered it a good possibility.[2] Today, more than a decade later, the figures have no doubt jumped considerably, and it would be reasonable to extrapolate that almost one-third of the populace of many Western nations entertain some version of reincarnation. However, the conception of reincarnation in the West is considerably different from its conception in the Orient.

Eastern and Western Views of Reincarnation Contrasted
In the Orient reincarnation is viewed as an overwhelming fact of life, although a lamentable one. In one way or another, it conditions almost every traditionally religious Asian. The Asian view often sees life as a dreary burden, a

state of affairs to be endured. "The wheel of rebirth and suffering" is a phrase often used in the Orient; and rebirth simply means more hard times, not a wonderful and bounteous opportunity. Undoubtedly this is directly connected to the sheer difficulty of physical existence for many Asians.

This pessimistic view of life has its roots in antiquity. Guatama Buddha's central concern was the problem of pain and suffering. He taught that the source of the human predicament lies in the attachment of the mind and body to the physical realm or, more precisely, to existence itself. Hence the logical solution is to cease existing and, of course, to stop being reborn. In fact, the Buddhist word for "heaven"—*nirvana*—literally means "blown out," like a candle. In his teachings on such abstract metaphysics, Buddha never mentioned God; for him, "God" was merely cause and effect. Because of this doctrine, Buddhism has often been called "the atheistic religion."

However, the view held by current Western reincarnationists is markedly different. Their view has been shaped out of a different cultural and philosophic outlook, an outgrowth of two thousand years of Christian thought. After paganism and the mystery religions died out and Christianity gained the upper hand in the fourth century, the Christian teaching of resurrection became the clear consensus in Europe as well as in those parts of the world influenced by Islam, which, since it draws on biblical thought, also teaches resurrection.

The term *resurrection* has somewhat different connotations in various religious traditions. In its broadest use, resurrection may be defined as an awakening after death to a life in the presence of God or, in polytheistic religions, with the gods. In contrast to the reincarnated soul, the resurrected soul does not return again to earth in a different body.

Immortality of the Soul

The biblical idea of resurrection should not, however, be

confused with this generalized concept of resurrection nor with the Platonic idea of immortality of the soul. The doctrine of immortality of the soul assumes that the soul is a substance trapped in the body. It is the "true self," or life essence, and is not to be confused with the personality surrounding a particular body. The soul is held to be capable of independent, disembodied existence. Central to the Christian concept of immortality, however, is its concept that the resurrection of the soul is not ultimately distinct from that of the body (or at least it is not complete without the body); "the resurrection of the body" was a cardinal tenet of the early church and was written into the creeds. This resurrection of the body, of course, is not a body of flesh as we know it, but a spiritual body such as the apostle Paul describes in 1 Corinthians 15; it is nonetheless a real body, and it retains the personality and identity of the one who died. Theologian Carl Henry elaborates: "Loss of this hope of bodily resurrection brings with it the loss of any expectation whatever of an afterlife. . . . The afterlife is not some kind of a fragmented existence, moreover, but includes life in a body. . . . Life as a disembodied spirit is neither ideal nor normal for man, and awaits being clothed with the promised resurrection body."[3] The hope embodied in the biblical view of resurrection is inseparable from the Christian conviction that evil will be finally conquered and put away at the Second Coming of Christ and the Final Judgment.

Even though life in Christianized Europe was often dangerous and dreary, the knowledge that Christ had redeemed the world from everlasting slavery and the hope that life would culminate in the presence of God, as taught by Jesus and the New Testament writers, undergirded Western thought. This understanding supplied a foundation for an optimistic view of life—even for those who may not have been confessing Christians. Such optimism stands in marked contrast to the cyclic view of life held in the

East, where evil and suffering are an eternal status quo.

When the teaching of reincarnation was revived in the West during the Enlightenment of the eighteenth century and popularly propagated by such nineteenth-century occult movements as Theosophy, a strange philosophical hybrid began to flower in the soil of Judeo-Christian culture. Instead of viewing life as an eternal treadmill of sorrow, boredom and drudgery, as those in the Orient viewed it, Western reincarnationists extolled the joys of life on earth with optimistic pronouncements. Leoline Wright, in her book *Reincarnation,* writes: "All of us, undoubtedly, as Spiritual Egos have played many parts on this *wonderful* stage of human drama, our planet Earth" (emphasis mine).[4] Theosophist Joy Mills expands on this in speaking of *the law of karma* (which determines one's status in succeeding reincarnations): "The ramifications of the law must be as endless and complex as those processes; yet in its ultimate simplicity, the law finally is known as *love*" (emphasis mine).[5]

Such sentiments recur regularly in the writings of modern reincarnationists, who frequently trade the reality of suffering throughout the world for the hope of more and better lives. Transcendental Meditation's guru-founder Maharishi Mahesh Yogi, a modern proponent of reincarnation, observed this attitude of selective perception in the West when he said, "We must take our message to the West, to those who are in the habit of accepting things quickly!"[6]

Another reason for reincarnation's appeal in the West relates to its association with the New Age religious movements and their spin-offs, such as Erhard Seminars Training (est), Yoga, Zen and the occult counterculture belief that we are about to enter the astrological golden age, the Age of Aquarius. California hypnotherapist Dr. Helen Wambach, a proponent of New Age philosophy who specializes in hypnotically regressing people to alleged past lives, asked some of her subjects why they chose to incarnate at this time in history. They usually responded, "Because it is the New Age, the Aquarian Age, the time of transition for the human race."[7] Hence reincarnation appears to many as new and exciting, bearing overtones of exotic wisdom and "deeper truth."

Thus modern reincarnationists try to syncretize Eastern and Western beliefs, transplanting Hindu and Buddhist presuppositions into a largely Christianized culture. But it is a bit like trying to cross-fertilize apples with oranges. As Anglican churchman Michael Paternoster notes in a brief analysis of reincarnation, "If then, reincarnation is to be acclimatized to the Christian world, it will play a very different part from the one it plays in Indian religions."[8]

2

Reincarnation and Karma

SOME SCHOLARS DISTINGUISH between the concepts of reincarnation and rebirth. Reincarnation is more closely associated with Hindu tradition and suggests a retention of an individualized soul from one life to the next, although the former life is not usually remembered. Rebirth, on the other hand, is more congenial to Buddhism, with its emphasis on the transfer of an impersonal life force, much as one candle is lit from the flame of another. In any event, I will use the terms interchangeably both for the sake of convenience and also because almost all the secondary doctrines and semantic subtleties surrounding reincarnationist thought are subject to contradiction, debate and confusion.

The Movement of the Soul
Most traditions hold to a basic scenario which may be summarized thus: The "soul" enters the physical realm as a mineral or unicellular organism and then evolves upward through plant and animal lives until it reaches the ultimate physical state as a human being. Although there are excep-

tions, it is generally held that once a soul becomes human it cannot regress to a lower state. Despite the many variations in reincarnation philosophy, the following definition formulated by Theosophist Anna Winner, would find almost universal acceptance:

> The belief in reincarnation which is held by occultists is the belief that an individual human soul passes through a great number (many hundreds or thousands) of successive incarnations as a human being, with alternating periods in subtle worlds. . . . The individual is not specifically "created," but derives from the group soul by a natural process of "budding off."[1]

The "subtle worlds" to which Winner refers are the spirit realm in which the soul may spend time before its next arduous descent into the physical world. Theories vary widely on how long the stay in the spirit world is; some schools insist that reincarnation occurs within days or hours, while others say that it may delay for thousands of years. The Rosicrucians have concluded that "each Ego or personality reincarnates again on earth approximately every 144th year."[2] However, Dr. Ian Stevenson, who has researched hundreds of "spontaneous past-life recall" cases, reports that the time lapse between incarnations of subjects he has observed in India is five to ten years. Helen Wambach reports from her studies of over one thousand subjects an average time of fifty-one years between death and rebirth.

According to classical thought, the soul endures thousands of lives as a human being. Some of the soul's incarnations may even occur on other planets or in other solar systems. Certain schools even specify the number of years a soul must remain on earth; the well-known guru Paramhansa Yogananda cited an average of one million years. Elisabeth Kübler-Ross, an expert on death and dying who in recent years has devoted her attention to spiritualism, claims that her spirit guides divulged the following information to her: "God creates everybody to fulfill his destiny in one life time, but very few make it, perhaps one in a billion. The shortest time between the creation of a human being and his return to God was 43 years. The longest has been 2,000,000 years and he is still in this universe and has not made it yet. Just to give you some idea what the options are."[3]

Hinduism teaches that final liberation from the round of rebirths can only be achieved by humans. Only through the pitfalls and travails of the human condition can a soul earn sufficient merit to warrant its release or liberation (Sanskrit *moksha* or *samadhi*). Thus a soul must evolve through various life forms to the human state, the evolutionary plateau where moral lessons are learned through multitudes of reincarnations.

The big picture. On a macrocosmic scale, Hindus believe that the universe itself reincarnates in multibillion-year cycles. The universe begins as a state of pure "Unmanifest Absolute," that is, an incomprehensibly large vacuum which contains all the potential for creation. Within the vacuum an undefined imbalance, impulse or irrepressible desire to create and manifest causes the creation cycle to start, thus beginning "The Day of Brahm," in which the creative activity of the universe continues for billions of years. Finally all souls complete their multitudinous incarnations, attaining "enlightenment," and all is merged back into the primordial, universal vacuum state called "The Night of Brahm." This period also lasts billions of years. It should also be noted that *all* things in nature are subject to this cosmic recycling and evolution. As Madame Helena Petrovna Blavatsky, the founder of Theosophy, says, "The law of cause and effect applies to all depths of nature."[4]

Karma. The law of cause and effect to which Madame Blavatsky refers is called *karma*. She defines it in this way: "It is the power that controls all things," and "Deity is law and vice-versa." She then elaborates:

Karma simply means that there remains nought after each personality but the causes produced by it. No "personality"—a mere bunch of material atoms and of instinctual mental characteristics—can of course continue as such, in the world of pure Spirit.[5]

The fundamental idea behind karma is that of action followed by reaction. The Bhagavad-Gita, one of the best-known Hindu scriptures, defines it quite simply as "the name given to the creative force that brings beings into existence" (8:3). Thus, it may be viewed as the fundamental creative action which is perpetuated in each individual soul. Practically, karma is somewhat like Isaac Newton's law: For every action there is an equal and opposite reaction. It could be pictured as a set of moral scales; all the bad deeds piled up on one side must be balanced by good deeds on the other.

Yet it is more complicated than that. Perhaps the best way of picturing karma and its relationship to rebirth is something like this: Each person is a sort of electronic sensor or microphone with a wire hooked up to a great computer in the heavens; the computer is "God." Each thought, motive and act, as well as all the things that happen *to* us, are relayed back to the computer and filed away. Upon death the data bank in the computer is activated, and the "readout" of our next life, based on how we have balanced our karma in the preceding life or lives, is cranked out and handed to us. If our negative karma (deeds, thoughts, motives, circumstances, and so on) outweigh our positive karmic pattern, we are assigned a more miserable existence in the next round, and vice versa. We have nothing to say about it. There is no mercy, forgiveness or court of appeals.[6]

Admittedly, the computer story is my invention, but it is a substantially accurate analogy. Madame Blavatsky uses a similar idea:

Whenever and wherever imbalance is produced, the self-adjusting "mechanism" comes into play to restore equilibrium. . . . The karmic connection between lives is made by *skandhas*, bundles of attributes. They are psychomental link mechanisms by which characteristics are passed from one personality to its successors. They correspond to the DNA, gene, and chromosome arrangement of inherited qualities in the physical bodies.[7]

I have used Blavatsky (1831-91) as a source for definitions because the comparatively recent vintage of her writings reflects the refinement of Western expression and metaphors, and because she holds a dominant influence in contemporary metaphysical speculation. However, her interpretation of the finer details and convolutions of reincarnation doctrine and oriental philosophy is an eclectic blending of her own idiosyncrasies with Eastern sources, and many serious oriental scholars consider her a somewhat misguided charlatan. Many Buddhists, by contrast, hold that the karmic connection between incarnations is not specific; they use alternative conceptions, such as "thought forces" or "impersonal character," to account for karma and reincarnation.

Gnostic Philosophy and Mystical Experience

Whatever the ins and outs of the reincarnation cycles may be, the goal and purpose is to merge with God or the Cosmos or, more precisely, to *become* God so as to put an end to the painful cycle of rebirths. To this end Blavatsky comments, "It is owing to this law of spiritual development that mankind will become freed from its false gods and find itself finally—SELF REDEEMED" (emphasis hers).[8]

This sentiment of *cosmic humanism,* which places the autonomy of the human being at the center of things, is really the distilled essence of the philosophical system that undergirds all reincarnation teachings. Understanding this world view, which may be called "gnostic philosophy and mystical experience," is essential if we want to comprehend the doctrine of reincarnation. "Gnostic" comes from the Greek word *gnosis*, meaning "knowledge." This knowing is not necessarily knowledge in the scholarly sense; the heart of gnosis is *an intuitive and existential apprehension of the Cosmos and the Divine,* which are one and the same, for the universe *is* God. This knowledge can only be attained through *mystical experience,* that is, an altered state of consciousness wherein the person feels that he or she is one with, or joined to, the entire universe, or God.

Primarily then, gnosticism asserts the centrality, power, and inherent divinity of humanity, denies the idea of a sovereign personal God and condemns as obsolete any final statement of moral values.[9]

The four main points of gnostic doctrine (or "occult science" as it is sometimes called) taken in logical order fall in this sequence:

1. *All is One.* This is the proposition that all existence is of one basic essence which finds its lowest common denominator in the Eastern conception of Deity, the impersonal Absolute which is called *Brahman* in Sanskrit. Brahman is the metaphysical substratum of the universe, the cosmic field from which all possibilities arise. The unity of all things is the subjective revelation most commonly encountered in mystical experience. In common parlance, it is usually called *pantheism (pan,* "all"; *theos,* "God") or *monism (mono,* "one"). Fundamentally, the unity of all things means that God is not separate from creation.

2. *Humanity is essentially divine.* This is a logical inference from the first statement. If the universe is divine and human beings are a conscious part of that universe, they must also be divine, at least at their very core.

3. Therefore, *the purpose of life is to become experientially aware of our divine nature.* Salvation thus becomes the attainment of this reality through union with the Divine Absolute.

4. *Mastery of "spiritual technology" and mystical experience*

(for example, Yoga, meditation, magic ritual) *leads to the attainment of spiritual power.* Thus, the adept literally become the Creator, not merely by merging with God, but by creating their own reality through the power of a controlled mind. This state is "enlightenment," or salvation, and results in the cessation of the wheel of death and rebirth, or reincarnation.[10]

Whether or not they would verbalize it so systematically, all who are serious believers in reincarnation ultimately hold some form of this basic gnostic creed. It is the foundation on which the concept of reincarnation rests. If any Hindu or Buddhist ascetic who has renounced the world to sit in a cold Himalayan monastery for years on end is asked, "Why do you do it?" his predictable reply would be quickly forthcoming: "Because I'm tired of the pointless misery of suffering and rebirth, and I want to be released from the bondage of karma through mastery of spiritual techniques, austerities and meditation. I want this to be my last life."

3
A Short History of Reincarnation Teachings

Many early pagan religions held to some idea of resurrection, but the range of their conceptions is obscured by lack of original literature. Some ancients did hold to loosely defined concepts of spiritual change after death; in classical Greek mythology, for instance, Proteus could change his form at will. Though such ideas appear more closely allied to resurrection than to reincarnation, some of these early beliefs may have contained crude expressions of reincarnation.

Ancient Egypt

Many people have claimed that the ancient Egyptians taught reincarnation. This erroneous conclusion is based on references to Egyptian theories of transmigration of the soul made by ancient Greek writers. *The Egyptian Book of the Dead* speaks of the soul being able to change itself into various life forms after death. But this change is best understood as a sort of spiritual evolution in the heavenly realms, not a bodily return to this earth. James Henry

Breasted, professor of Egyptology at the University of Chicago, summed up the opinion of most Egyptologists when he said, "It was this notion which led Herodotus to conclude that the Egyptians believed in what we now call transmigration of souls, but this was a mistaken impression on his part."[1]

The ancient Egyptians certainly believed in an afterlife in another realm or world, but references to reincarnation in the traditional understanding are simply absent. The practice of mummification and the filling of the burial chamber with practical items and symbolic trinkets was intended to prepare the deceased for the next world, not a return to this one.

The East

The precise historical origins of reincarnation doctrines in the East are difficult to pin down because Eastern philosophy is less concerned with the history and dating of events than the West. The historical sequence of events matters little to those who view life as a repetition of eternal cycles and the physical world as illusion.

Despite this historical problem, it seems quite certain that the idea of reincarnation had its origin in the ancient speculative philosophies of India. Although some Hindu scholars insist that the oldest of the Hindu scriptures, the Vedas, teach reincarnation, no clear statement of the doctrine can be found in them. The majority of experts agree that the pervasive teaching of the Vedas is that of resurrection and immortality with the gods, similar to that which is found in other polytheistic religions of the time. On the whole, it would seem fair to suppose that if the early Vedas do not specifically define or speak of reincarnation, the idea was not taught by the early Aryans, who wrote these first Hindu scriptures.

Swami Agehananda Bharati, an Austrian by birth, was initiated into Hinduism in India in the early 1950s and is now professor of anthropology at Syracuse University. Fluent in a half-dozen Indian and Tibetan languages, Bharati is considered one of the leading Western experts on Hinduism and Buddhism. In an interview he gave the following responses to questions I asked about the history of reincarnation teachings:

Q: How old is the idea of reincarnation and where does it come from?

Bharati: In its present form, the way people talk about it today, it is quite old, but it's not as old as people hope it would be. You have only a vestigial or marginal mention of something like transmigration in the older sections of the Veda. There is the first complete mention, though very brief, in the Brihadaranyaka Upanishad, which is quite old. But the real assumptions having to do with reincarnation come in the Puranic age, at the time that the Puranas were composed, and then of course, through Buddhism. So you might say that it reached a state of common acceptance, I would think, around 300 B.C., but not earlier. So it is old, but in its highly articulated form it is not so old—and the way it's talked about now, that's recent; that's "Theosophical Society."

Q: What about early Greek thought? Do you find it in Plato, for instance?

Bharati: Earlier than that. Pythagoras. But again, it's not elaborated. You find traces of a metempsychotic statement [reincarnation] in Pythagoras, which is older than Socrates. But it was never taken too seriously. Also, it was not commonly accepted and did not become part and parcel of the Greek religious system at any time.[2]

R. C. Zaehner, the well-known oriental scholar from Oxford University, comments similarly:

Of this [reincarnation] there is no trace in the Samhitas or Brahmanas [earliest scriptures], and it is only when we come to the Upanishads that we first meet with this doctrine which was to become central to all Hindu thought. In the Rig Veda [earliest Veda] the soul of the dead is carried aloft by the fire-god, Agni, who consumes the material body at cremation, to the heavenly worlds where it disports itself with the gods in perfect, carefree bliss. There will be eating and drinking of heavenly food and drink, reunion with father, mother, wife and sons. In the Brihadaranyaka Upanishad (6. 2. 15-16), however, a distinction is made. Purified by the fire that has consumed their gross bodies, they pass on into the flame, the day, the world of the gods, and hence into the lightning. A spiritual person conducts them into the worlds of Brahman. Of these there is no return. They have achieved eternal bliss. The followers of the sacrificial cult, however, pass on into smoke, the night, the world of the fathers, and finally into the moon. There they become the food of the gods, "but when that passes away from them, they descend into space, from space into the air, from air into the rain, and from rain into the earth. When they reach the earth they become food. Once again they are offered as an oblation in the fire of a man. and thence they are born in the fire of a woman. Rising up into the worlds, they circle round within them. But those who do not know these two ways, become worms, moths, and biting serpents." Here for the first time we meet the doctrine of rebirth.[3]

Thus, the idea of resurrection does seem to predate reincarnation. But a fully developed and popular doctrine of reincarnation seems to have been flourishing by about 300 B.C., and perhaps earlier than that. It is more apparent in the later scriptures, such as the late Upanishads and especially the semicanonical Bhagavad-Gita. The Bhagavad-Gita, probably rewritten or edited since the time of Christ, refers pointedly to reincarnation. Krishna says to Arjuna, the hero of this popular Indian epic: "Just as a person casts off worn-out garments and puts on others that are new, even so does the embodied soul cast off worn-out bodies and take on others that are new" (2. 22).

In Hinduism, the Sanskrit word *samsara* is usually employed when speaking of the cycle of karma and rebirth. In fact, it is so prevalent that it is not really taught as a doctrine subject to debate. It is simply taken for granted by all Hindus as a law which governs life, much like gravity. In his book, *The Tantric Tradition,* Bharati points out that there are only two universally accepted presuppositions in Indian religion. One is the concept of the Brahman, and the other is reincarnation.

Rebirth has always been an integral part of Buddhism as well, although as previously noted, the imagery is somewhat different. While speculation about reincarnation seems to have been fairly common among philosophers and sages in the Buddha's day (ca. 500 B.C.), it is uncertain whether he actually believed in its reality, except as an ethical concept or as the continuance of the life force in an abstract sense. Classical Buddhist doctrine postulates the existence of *skandhas,* which are unrelated psychic "causes" that are dissolved upon death and reactivated at birth. However, this is different from the Hindu concept of an individual soul reincarnating; it is more impersonal. Each individual is born with characteristics from a variety of past lives and other karmic sources, just as an automobile might be assembled from miscellaneous parts in a junkyard. The Buddha was therefore rather circumspect when discussing the particulars of reincarnation, as may be observed in this quotation from the Majjhima Nikaya:

I have not elucidated that the world is eternal, and I have not elucidated that the world is not eternal. I have not elucidated that the saint exists after death, I have not elucidated that the saint does not exist after death. I have not elucidated that the saint both exists and does not exist after death.[4]

In early Chinese religion and philosophy a similar problem is encountered. Although reincarnation is generally accepted in Taoism, its founder, the philosopher Lao-tse (ca. 604-531 B.C.), did not specifically teach it. Lao-tse's distant disciple Chuang-tzu (ca. 300 B.C.) did teach the doctrine, so it would appear that reincarnationist thought developed in China at about the same time it was being accepted in India.

The Middle East

Some references to reincarnation can be found in Zoroastrianism (Persian dualism), which flourished as early as the seventh century B.C., and in Mithraism. Mithraism was typical of the host of "mystery religions" which resulted from the social and political upheavals that followed in the wake of Alexander the Great's colonization of the eastern Mediterranean. Many ethnic and religious groups were uprooted and brought into contact with others as the Middle East became more cosmopolitan. The resultant melting pot acted as a crucible which forged new religious movements with occult and syncretistic overtones, blended with Greek and Persian philosophy. In many respects these cults were expanded versions of indigenous variations or tribal expressions of pantheistic shamanism, the "witch doctor" religions of spirit worship or pantheism that are common to almost all areas of the globe. A crude form of reincarnation or rebirth was (and still is) a fairly common belief in some of these primitive shamanistic systems. (Good examples can still be found in Africa, the South Pacific, rural Asia and even Alaska.)

Islam, which arose some six centuries after Christ, is derived largely from biblical thought and history. As a result the orthodox mainstream of Islam has disavowed reincarnation, adhering to the Judeo-Christian concept of resurrection. However, the mystical wing of Islam, the Sufis, who incorporate considerable oriental teaching and practice into their Muslim faith, have been believers in reincarnation since their inception. The Sufis notwithstanding, rebirth is not taught in the Islamic scriptures, the Koran, and Muslims generally disavow the notion of reincarnation.

Western Roots

Some of the surviving literature from pre-Christian Europe also suggests reincarnational thinking. The original settlers of northern and central Europe, such as the Teutons, Celts and Druids, had fairly sophisticated religious systems which were probably influenced by classical Greece, where religious speculation and philosophy were honed to a razor's edge. W. Bryher notes in the foreword to *Ruan* that "we know something of Celtic doctrine from early Welsh poetry and Breton folklore. It seems to have had much in common with some forms of eastern thought. Life was considered as a time of trial: if its initiation was successfully passed, the spirit rested after death until the moment came for another return to earth. This continued until, after many lives some attained to the state of spiritual perfection."[5]

"That ancient doctrine."   Plato used reincarnation concepts as a literary device in his stories and writings. Whether or not he actually believed the doctrine may never be known, but it was undoubtedly a popular and widely entertained belief in his time—and he got plenty of mileage from it. His doctrine of the immortality of the soul and the soul's de-identification with the body certainly encouraged speculation about reincarnation, or "transmigration of souls" as it was known to the Greeks. He speaks of it by quoting his mentor, Socrates (d. 399 B.C.), who referred to it laconically as "that ancient doctrine."

Since Socrates called reincarnation an ancient doctrine (if Plato's quotation is to be taken at face value), it would seem that ideas of rebirth find their genesis sometime before 500 B.C., at least in the cruder and speculative formulations. While it is virtually impossible to put a date on the exact beginning of *coherent* reincarnation teachings, 1000 B.C. would be a generous estimate for the date of its Indian roots, with 800-600 B.C. being perhaps closer to the mark. In any event, the evidence clearly indicates that it was a *speculative philosophy* that developed primarily around the Hindu scriptures, the best example of which is the Brihadaranyaka Upanishad.

Further developments. After Greek influence in the West faded with the demise of Alexander the Great's empire, the reincarnation torch passed to the Romans, where it was held aloft by the influential Stoics; by the time the Roman Empire hit its peak, the entire Mediterranean area was heavily influenced by the Neo-Platonism of Plotinus and others. This philosophy of the sophisticated and erudite ancients was mixed in varying proportions with the mystery religions, influences from Persia and India, plus elements from the Greek and Roman pantheon. On the spiritual outskirts were the Gnostics, who attempted to reduce Christianity to just another mystery religion with Jesus as the leader. Relying heavily on esoteric, "secret" interpretations of the Bible, Gnosticism taught a vague form of rebirth, although it was merely a secondary doctrine. Gnosticism became the major external challenge to the early church, as we shall see in chapter four.

Despite the influence of Christendom, which has dominated Western civilization since the time of Christ, the mystical and occultic traditions have periodically raised their heads in Europe, notably in such groups as the Hermetic Orders, Albigenses, Cathari and Knights Templars.[6] Finally, gnostic occultism made a substantial comeback in Europe and the United States in the nineteenth century with the founding of the Theosophical Society, the influence of the American transcendentalists (for example, Emerson and Thoreau) and the arrival of Hindu Vedanta philosophy promoted by the Ramakrishna Mission and Swami Vivekananda.

The slowly ripening fruit of the esoteric "tree of knowledge" has nearly arrived at harvest time. The many gurus, "enlightened masters," holistic health centers, mediums and seances, parapsychology groups, spirit communications, witchcraft, numerous Eastern cults, Yoga and Zen have all espoused some form of gnostic philosophy and mystical experience as their unifying metaphysic, and reincarnation is certainly a basic tenet in this latest revival of ancient speculation.

The historic train of gnostic and pantheistic influence is succinctly traced and summed up by the well-known Christian writer C. S. Lewis:

> Pantheism is congenial to our minds not because it is the final stage in a slow process of enlightenment, but because it is almost as old as we are. It may even be the most primitive of all religions. . . . It is immemorial in India. The Greeks rose above it only at their peak; . . . their successors relapsed into the great Pantheistic system of the Stoics. Modern Europe escaped it only while she remained predominantly Christian; with Giordano Bruno and Spinoza it returned. With Hegel it became almost the agreed philosophy of highly educated people. . . . So far from being the final religious refinement, Pantheism is in fact the permanent natural bent of the human mind; the permanent ordinary level below which man sometimes sinks, . . . but above which his own unaided efforts can never raise him for very long. . . . It is the attitude into which the human mind automatically falls when left to itself. No wonder we find it congenial. If "religion" means simply what man says about God, and not what God does about man, then Pantheism *is* religion. And "religion" in that sense has, in the long run, only one really formidable opponent—namely Christianity.[7]

4

Reincarnation in the Bible and the Early Church

Proponents of Reincarnation adamantly insist that their doctrine was taught by both Jesus and the early church and that the Bible teaches it as well. If they are right, then C. S. Lewis's contention that Christianity is a foe of pantheism is mistaken, for, as we saw in chapter two, reincarnationist thought depends ultimately on the pantheistic presuppositions of gnosticism.

But the problem goes deeper than that. If reincarnation is (or was) a central part of the original Christian gospel, then historic, orthodox Christianity has veered significantly from its original course. Historic orthodoxy has vigorously denied reincarnation for two principal reasons. First, Christianity has taught a doctrine of resurrection: the human soul does not return to earth after death, but is resurrected as an individual personality to face judgment. Second, it has taught that God forgives and extends mercy in the face of human sin and shortcomings. There is no forgiveness and little, if any, mercy connected with the idea of reincarnation. Each soul pays the inevitable price for its own failings and misdeeds, in hundreds or thousands of existences.

Reincarnation and the Bible
Many people insist that the Bible teaches reincarnation, citing a number of obscure verses, always out of context and buttressed by explanatory comments which have highly dubious exegetical roots. However, only four of these texts are really significant and deserving of exploration. Three are sayings from Jesus himself, and the fourth is found in the epistle of James.

The first passage, in the third chapter of John's Gospel, the contextual problem of reading reincarnation into the New Testament is well illustrated. In verse three Jesus, addressing Nicodemus, says according to some translations, "Unless one is born again, he cannot see the kingdom of God." Some reincarnationists insist that by the phrase "born again" Jesus was teaching reincarnation. The Greek word *anōthen,* here translated "again," can also be rendered "above," which would make the phrase read "born from above." The context holds the key to the meaning, and it shows that Jesus was speaking of spiritual rebirth in this life as a precondition for eternal life. In fact, Nicodemus asked him further, "How can a man be born when he is old? Can he enter a second time into his mother's womb and be born?" (v. 4). The questions indicate that Nicodemus understood Jesus to be speaking of some kind of re-birth in this life, not any form of reincarnation, which would have been a foreign concept in first-century Judaism. "Jesus answered, 'Truly, truly, I say to you, unless one is born of water and the Spirit, he cannot enter the kingdom of God' " (v. 5). Thus the thrust of this statement about being born again is connected with the frequent New Testament proclamation that salvation had to be accomplished through *spiritual* regeneration, that is, conversion and repentance. This theme is repeated so often by Jesus that it becomes virtually impossible to construe this text as speaking of reincarnation.

Who was John the Baptist?   The next and most complicated passage has to do with John the Baptist and Elijah. The common Jewish belief at the time was that Elijah would return to "restore all things" before the Messiah appeared, a belief that Jesus affirmed. Jesus makes three statements about John the Baptist in the Gospels which could be understood as references to reincarnation. The first is Matthew 11:14: "If you are willing to accept it, he [John] is Elijah who is to come." Later in Matthew 17:12-13, Jesus again said, " 'But I tell you that Elijah has already come, and they [the Jews] did not know him, but did to him whatever they pleased. So also the Son of man will suffer at their hands.' Then the disciples understood that he was speaking to them of John the Baptist." In Mark 9:13 the same theme is echoed. "But I tell you that Elijah has come, and they did to him whatever they pleased, as it is written of him."

So it seems that Elijah had indeed come back, according to Jesus: "as it is written of him." The central question then is *how* did he come back? Jesus' reference to biblical prophecy in Mark 9:13 is found in the book of Malachi: "I send my messenger to prepare the way before me" (3:1) and "Behold, I will send you Elijah the prophet before the great and terrible day of the LORD comes" (4:5). The angel who appeared to Zechariah announcing John the Baptist's birth elaborated on these statements: "And he [John] will go before him [Jesus] in the spirit and power of Elijah" (Lk 1:17). The angel did not tell Zechariah that his son was to be Elijah reincarnate.

After John the Baptist began his ministry, the public was confused about his identity. In an attempt to settle the matter, the Jewish religious leaders sent a delegation of priests and Levites from Jerusalem to confront John. They asked him, " 'Who are you? . . . Are you Elijah?' He said, '*I am not.* . . . I am the voice of one crying in the wilderness, "Make

straight the way of the Lord," as the prophet Isaiah said' "
(Jn 1:19-23). John's denial is crucial; we also must note that
Jesus did not say "John the Baptist is Elijah," nor did he
mention reincarnation in dealing with the issue. Rather, we
are looking at a classic example of biblical typology; that
is, John the Baptist was a "type" of Elijah. He fulfilled the
role of Elijah, as prophesied by Malachi. John the Baptist
had the same endowment of power and spiritual characteristics as Elijah. This is stated most explicitly in the quotation
from Luke, that John would "go before him *in the spirit and
power* of Elijah."

One other point should be noted: In reincarnation doctrine death must precede rebirth and Elijah never died.
According to 2 Kings 2:11, Elijah was taken up "by a whirlwind into heaven." Finally, it is significant that when Elijah
reappeared with Moses on the Mount of Transfiguration
(Mt 17 and Mk 9), there was no confusion among the disciples as to who he was. They immediately recognized both
Moses and Elijah, and they did not confuse either of them
with John the Baptist.

The "cycle of nature." A third text found in the Bible
with marginal reincarnational overtones is the reference
in James 3:6 to the "cycle of nature," which can be literally
rendered "wheel of genesis," a phrase suggestive of Buddhism. In this passage the apostle James is comparing the
human tongue to a fire, a fire that touches the whole body
and inflames the whole cycle of life, as rash and thought-
less language embodies the sins and passions of the human
condition. Hence he is referring to the sinful state of the
human race and the role of the tongue (speech) as the most
obvious outworking of our fallen condition. Ronald Ward
in *The New Bible Commentary: Revised* says of the passage:

> The tongue inflames *the cycle of nature, i.e.* "the wheel of
> *genesis*" (*cf.* on 1:23). We can dismiss doctrines of reincar-
> nation from the exposition of the robust Jewish Christian
> James. He loosely uses a Hellenistic expression associ-

ated with the Orphic mysteries and ultimately with Indian thought. It seems to mean here "course of life." Now the tongue is concerned with communication. Each speaker may be seen standing in *the cycle* or "circle" of humanity and *setting* it *on fire* with desire, suspicion, rivalry, hatred and war. (Ward's emphasis)[1]

Did the blind man live before? Last, there is the revealing passage in John 9:1-3 about the man born blind.

> As he [Jesus] passed by, he saw a man blind from his birth. And his disciples asked him, "Rabbi, who sinned, this man or his parents, that he was born blind?" Jesus answered, "It was not that this man sinned, or his parents, but that the works of God might be made manifest in him."

The disciples were wrestling with the eternal question of seemingly unjust circumstances: a man with a severe birth defect lay at their feet. In probing Jesus as to the reason for these sad circumstances, they ask him what seems to be a double-barreled question, "Who sinned, *this man* or *his parents,* that he was born blind?"

The implications of the first half of the question seem obvious enough within the context of reincarnationist speculation. As has been noted, rebirth doctrines were circulating in New Testament times, and the disciples, who were caught up in the spiritual whirlwind of speculation that surrounded Jesus, may well have considered theories of reincarnation. While it cannot be said with certainty that the disciples were referring to rebirth, it seems a likely explanation. How else could this man have "sinned," since he had been *born* blind?

The second half of the question centered on the Jewish concept that guilt was passed down several generations, and the possibility that the blind man was paying for his parents' or grandparents' transgressions.

Jesus' answer was direct and without hesitation: "It was *not that this man sinned or his parents,* but that the works of

God might be made manifest in him." Having said that, Jesus healed him, and the man then glorified God and worshiped Jesus. If reincarnation was believed and taught by Jesus, this would have been the ideal opportunity to explain the doctrines of karma and reincarnation; yet with one sentence, he apparently excluded it as a possible explanation.

In Luke's Gospel there is a similar passage which implicitly excludes karma and reincarnation as an explanation for seeming injustice in this life. Luke picks up the narrative and writes, "There were some present at that very time who told [Jesus] of the Galileans whose blood Pilate had mingled with their sacrifices. And [Jesus] answered them,

Do you think that these Galileans were worse sinners than all the other Galileans, because they suffered thus? I tell you, No; but unless you repent you will all likewise perish. Or those eighteen upon whom the tower in Siloam fell and killed them, do you think that they were worse offenders than all the others who dwelt in Jerusalem? I tell you, No; but unless you repent you will all likewise perish." (13:1-5)

Indeed, it is this biblical silence on the subject of reincarnation that is the real key to understanding the Christian attitude toward rebirth. While all the Eastern, gnostic and occult traditions enumerate karmic patterns and the destiny of rebirth with detail and precision, it is never mentioned in the Bible, which refers only to resurrection. Geddes MacGregor, distinguished professor emeritus of philosophy at the University of Southern California, is a Christian who believes that a subdued or modified form of reincarnation can conceivably be grafted on to Christianity. But he too admits in his book *Reincarnation in Christianity* that "the Bible does not explicitly teach reincarnationism."[2] Commenting further, he says, "Reincarnation was certainly not part of the principal ideological furniture of the Bible as it was of the literature of India that was the heritage of Buddha."[3] Furthermore, although reincarnation is never mentioned in the Bible, many biblical passages implicitly deny it.[4]

Reincarnation and the Early Church

Some modern reincarnationists suggest that the Bible does not explicitly teach reincarnation because the church in its historical development eliminated the teaching. Joseph Head and S. L. Cranston, in their anthology on rebirth titled *Reincarnation: The Phoenix Fire Mystery,* allege that "the New Testament was not recorded until long after Jesus died, and its books subsequently passed through the censoring hand of church councils. In the sixth and later centuries when the present Bible was decided on, a number of differing gospels existed. Those deemed unacceptable were destroyed."[5]

Did the original Bible get censored?   The charge made by Head and Cranston is a common one, but it is based on an erroneous view of early Christianity. The debate about the date of the New Testament composition has now been largely resolved and laid to rest by the consensus of New Testament scholarship. The overwhelming majority of biblical scholars—both liberal and conservative—now date the writing of the entire New Testament in the latter half of the first century. John A. T. Robinson, a noted British scholar of liberal persuasion, believes that the New Testament canon was written by A.D. 70. Although most scholars would date the Gospel of John and the Revelation twenty years later, we may be quite certain that the entire New Testament was either written by eyewitnesses to Jesus' ministry or compiled from eyewitness accounts. Such origins ensure the historicity of the Scriptures, especially the four Gospels.

During the first and second centuries the Gospels and Epistles were widely disseminated among the Christian churches of the Mediterranean world. After a short time there was considerable consensus about which writings were inspired and original and which were not. The criteria employed by the postapostolic church were three:

1. *Apostolicity.* Was the material written by an apostle? If not, did the writer (for example, Luke) have apostolic sanction? This sanction sometimes took the form of second-hand writing; that is, it may have been produced by an apostle's understudy, disciple or even an amanuensis (scribe).

2. *Doctrinal orthodoxy.* Did the writing contain the true teaching of the apostles? This could be determined quite easily through comparison with other apostolic writings and the oral tradition perpetuated in apostolic circles.

3. *Public reading.* Those documents which were consistently read as divine revelation in the majority of the churches in time came to be accepted as inspired. Thus by the end of the second century the canonical writings had gained widespread acceptance.[6] From an early date they were often quoted side by side with the Old Testament as Scripture (see 2 Pet 3:16).

A "hammering out process" followed for some years, during which period questions were raised over a handful of books such as Hebrews, James, 3 John, Jude and Revelation. Some minor variations in the number of books used in the local congregations occurred as late as the fourth century, but nothing hinting of Gnostic teaching was allowed or used in the apostolic churches at any time.

Many other writings existed and were given careful consideration, and even some popular orthodox writings, such as *The Didache* and *The Shepherd of Hermas,* were eliminated. Most of the New Testament apocrypha (noncanonical writings and gospels) are still extant and readily available; they have recently been subjected to considerable critical scholarship. It has now been established that these apocryphal gospels, mostly Gnostic in origin, were written in the second and third centuries, usually as extrapolations from or additions to the original four Gospels of Matthew, Mark, Luke and John. Thus the New Testament apocrypha were all written one to two hundred years after the departure of Christ from the world and could not have been written by eyewitnesses, which is a severe blow to their credibility.

We may therefore rest assured that we have in our present canon an accurate portrayal of the life and teachings of Jesus as well as a trustworthy interpretation of his ministry by the apostles in their subsequent writings, the Epistles, since Christ tacitly made provision for the writing of the New Testament by giving his authority to the apostles (see Mt 16:19). After the apostles died, the apostolic succession was handled with utmost care and a strong concern for the preservation of Christ's true teachings.

Was there an unwritten, secret teaching of Christ? The charge that the true esoteric doctrines of Christ have been suppressed is an old accusation which was first put forth by some of the Gnostic sects in the second century and was refuted at that time. The great apologist Irenaeus of Lyons, who was taught by Polycarp of Smyrna (a disciple of the apostle John), addressed this problem in *Against Heresies* about A.D. 190: "Even if the Apostles had known of hidden mysteries, which they taught to the perfect secretly and apart from others, they would have handed them down, especially to those to whom they were entrusting the churches themselves."[7]

Nevertheless, two Theosophist writers state that the early Christians had freely held reincarnational views until certain church councils decided otherwise.

It was not until some five centuries after the origin of Christianity, when it had long been the state religion of Rome, that the belief in reincarnation was formally declared to be not according to orthodox dogma.[8]

Reincarnation was accepted by some of the church fathers and prevailed so widely in early Christendom that as late as the middle of the sixth century after Christ it was necessary to convene a special Church Council in order finally to suppress it.[9]

The above writers refer to unnamed church councils, presumably presided over by elderly churchmen who, with a predisposition toward entrenched dogmatism, anathematized the doctrine of reincarnation. In fact, there was no such action at any church council in the entire first millennium: the subject was not even broached at the ecumenical councils. The only time a similar problem came up was in reference to the third-century theologian Origen, whose speculations concerning the pre-existence of the soul were anathematized at the Council of Constantinople in 553. However, Origen specifically denied reincarnation in his later writings (see page 46).

Reincarnation proponents sometimes fall into the trap of intellectual dishonesty before they realize it has closed over them: one cannot condemn the Bible as an edited compilation of the church fathers on the one hand, as Head and Cranston do, and then proceed to take portions of it out of context to prove rebirth theories on the other. If the church fathers had decided to extirpate reincarnation from the Bible, they would certainly have removed Jesus' statements about John the Baptist and Elijah. The argument that reincarnation is found in the Bible is sharply at odds with the parallel assertion of many reincarnationists that it was taken out of the Bible or anathematized at certain church councils. Reincarnationists cannot have it both ways.

Did the early church teach reincarnation? We have observed that reincarnationist teachings were woven into the spiritual fabric of the first- and second-century Hellenistic society in which the church was formed. This was due to earlier Platonic and Indian influence. A Buddhist king of India, Asoka, is said to have sent missionaries to the Mediterranean in the fourth century B.C.; and when this influence combined with Greek speculations, many mystery cults, as well as Gnosticism, flourished. Church historian

Kenneth Scott Latourette cites an example of such cultic teaching, which formed the spiritual milieu around the early church:

Various sects associated with the name of Orpheus held that matter and flesh are evil and that the soul of man must be free from contamination with them. They also taught that men are born and reborn, in each reincarnation imprisoned in the flesh and subject to those ills to which flesh is heir, unless the soul can be freed from the body. The separation accomplished, the soul would live forever in bliss. The emancipation was to be achieved through initiation into the cult, with cleanliness and asceticism.[10]

Confronted with such ideas, the early church persistently struggled to maintain its unique identity and teachings. Many gentile converts to the Christian faith had a subtle (or overt) mental preconditioning that was steeped in Greek philosophy, Gnosticism or mystery religions. Pagan converts often were influenced by the idea that the soul and body were in conflict with each other, leading to mystical speculations and practices, whereas Jewish thought had always perceived body and soul as a unity. As a result, Gentiles often had a difficult time with the Jewish heritage and Old Testament concepts that were pivotal to a correct understanding of Christianity. There is no question that these subtle influences crept into the church repeatedly and had to be dealt with. The apostle Paul concentrated on this problem in his letter to the Colossians as well as other New Testament epistles.

But did the Fathers themselves ever espouse reincarnation theories? Three in particular have been upheld as teaching such views: Justin Martyr, Origen and Jerome.

Justin Martyr. There are a number of statements made by contemporary reincarnationists about Justin Martyr (ca. 100-165), one of the church's first apologists. An anonymous British clergyman writes: "There is no doubt that many of the Christian Fathers held to [reincarnation] or were more or less disposed to it. Justin Martyr expressly speaks of the soul inhabiting more than one human body, and says that souls which fail in their duty pass into grosser forms."[11] The writer here takes his opinion from Justin's *Dialogue with Trypho,* issued about 155, some twenty years after his Disputation with Trypho the Jew, in which Justin had engaged shortly after his conversion. In this text Justin and Trypho discuss transmigration at some length and conclude that it is not such a good idea:

> **Trypho:** Therefore souls neither see God nor transmigrate into other bodies.
>
> **Justin:** You speak the truth, I agree.[12]

Origen. The greatest debate on the subject of reincarnation in the early church has raged around Origen (185-254). Head and Cranston state categorically, "That Origen taught the pre-existence of the soul in past world orders of this earth and its reincarnation in future worlds is beyond question."[13]

One of the great thinkers of early Christianity, Origen won by his speculative brilliance both admirers and antagonists within the church. Strongly influenced by Greek philosophy, Origen (at least in his earlier works) did teach the doctrine of pre-existence of the soul, that is, that humans were formerly angelic creatures whose good or bad deeds in the heavens resulted in a favorable or not-so-favorable birth on earth. His writings on pre-existence, however, specifically denied transmigration after the initial incarnation of the soul. Even many Christian scholars are unsure as to whether or not Origen held to reincarnation, but it would seem that they have simply not read Origen thoroughly on this subject. In his commentary on Matthew, he directly considers this under the title "Relation of John the Baptist to Elijah—the Theory of Transmigration Considered":

> In this place, it does not appear to me that by Elijah the soul is spoken of, lest I should fall into the dogma

of transmigration, which is foreign to the Church of God and not handed down by the Apostles, nor anywhere set forth in the Scriptures. For observe, [Matthew] did not say, in the "soul" of Elijah, in which case the doctrine of transmigration might have some ground, but "in the spirit and power of Elijah."[14]

In another place he says, "Let others who are strangers to the doctrine of the Church, assume that souls pass from the bodies of men into the bodies of dogs. We do not find this at all in the Divine Scriptures."[15] His commentary on Matthew was written toward the end of his life (about 247), when he was over sixty years of age, and it undoubtedly records his final opinions on the subject. His comments on John the Baptist and Elijah are followed by a lengthy refutation of the doctrine of transmigration.

Jerome. It is alleged that Jerome, a fourth-century saint and noted linguist, also promoted reincarnation. David Christie-Murray, in his book *Reincarnation: Ancient Beliefs and Modern Evidence,* asserts that "St. Jerome is supposed to have supported reincarnation in his 'Letter to Avitus' and that the doctrine was propounded among early Christians as an esoteric doctrine. Jerome was also a translator and admirer of Origen."[16]

Actually Jerome's letter to Avitus severely criticizes Origen for his Platonic ideas and nowhere condones the teaching of reincarnation. In his *Letter to Demetrius* he also refutes Origen's teaching on pre-existence, calling Origen's literary perambulations "a fountainhead of gross impiety."

Other notable Fathers. A number of other early Christian writers, indulging in the sarcasm and polemics common at that time, commented on transmigration. Irenaeus devoted the entirety of chapter thirty-three of *Against Heresies* to transmigration; his chapter title sets the tone: "Absurdity of the Doctrine of Transmigration of Souls."

Tertullian, the brilliant theologian and lawyer from Carthage, writing in his *Apology,* traces the doctrine of reincarnation to Pythagoras (ca. 450 B.C.) and opines that "the doctrine of transmigration is a falsehood which is not only shameful, but also hazardous. It is indeed manifest that dead men are formed from living ones; but it does not follow from that, that living men are formed from dead ones."[17]

Writing about "the fabulous doctrines of the heathen," Gregory of Nyssa (335-95), one of the most original thinkers of the young church, says:

> They tell us that one of their sages said that he, being one and the same person, was born a man, and afterwards assumed the form of a woman, and flew about with the birds, and grew as a bush, and obtained the life of an aquatic creature. And he who said these things of himself did not, so far as I can judge, go far from the truth: for such doctrines as this, saying that one soul passed through so many changes, are really fitting for the chatter of frogs and jackdaws, the stupidity of fishes, or the insensibility of trees.[18]

The heart of the matter seems to be that reincarnation was never much of a problem or issue in the early church. Even Augustine, despite the fact that he was a Manichaean Gnostic for nine years before his conversion and was well versed in Platonic thought, only mentions reincarnation in passing. In his letter to Optatus, he writes, "For it is impossible that you should hold the opinion that it is for deeds in a former life that souls are confined in earthly and mortal bodies."[19]

Other Christian writers such as Lactantius and Minucius Felix also mention and condemn transmigration. While it was occasionally addressed, no extant literature from the early ecumenical councils indicates that it was ever an issue for early Christianity. Although taught by a variety of non-Christian thinkers like the Neo-Platonists, reincarnation never was a part of the early church. Origen's theories on pre-existence might have easily developed into a full-blown incorporation of transmigratory speculations, but it seems that his teachings on this subject were never given serious credence.

One of the chief reasons for the early Christians' resistance to reincarnation was that the first-century church was rooted in the thought of Judaism, which had never embraced any systematic rebirth formulations. As MacGregor notes, "Though the Christian hope of resurrection is specifically allied to belief in the resurrection of Christ, the way had already been prepared for the resurrection idea by its development in late pre-Christian Jewish thought."[20]

The Kingdom of God

The message of Jesus as proclaimed in the Gospels can be summed up in four words: the kingdom of God. This phrase, or variations of it such as "kingdom of heaven" or simply "the kingdom," occurs seventy-four times in the four Gospels. The use of this phrase within the context of the Old Testament, first-century Judaism and the rest of the New Testament meant that God's rule would end the present worldly system of oppression, suffering, evil and chaos. The kingdom of God was to be a restoration of the fallen world, a miraculous transformation achieved by the appearance and action of God—in short, the end of the world as we know it. Jewish apocalyptic literature was in full flower at this time, pointing to the hope of the coming of the Messiah. Jesus made it very clear that his appearance was the long-awaited inbreaking of God's redemption and that he was the Messiah, who had come not to establish an earthly kingdom with its capital in Jerusalem, but to establish God's spiritual kingdom by conquering sin and death through his death and resurrection. The Jewish religious establishment did not understand this, and so they crucified him for blasphemy, since he had proclaimed himself equal to God; they never thought he would rise from the dead to vindicate his claims.

When Jesus rose on the first Easter Sunday, evil had been conquered on the cross and God's "beachhead" in the world had been established. Oscar Cullmann has observed that the resurrection was comparable to D-Day at Normandy in 1944; V-Day will occur when Jesus returns in the glory of the clouds to judge the world and restore the kingdom of God in fullness. Thus the early church had no concept of eternal cycles where good and evil would wax and wane. They thought in linear terms; the fallen status quo would be done away with *forever* at Christ's Second Coming.

Because of this, the real attitude of the early church toward reincarnation was not so much hostility as it was apathy. To the average Christian, reincarnation—if it was ever discussed—was fundamentally irrelevant. As MacGregor points out: "In Christian thought, reincarnation might [hypothetically] have occurred in the past; it could not occur in this world in the future, since there was to be no such world."[21]

This feeling was connected with the early church's hope that the end was at hand and that the Lord's Second Coming was imminent. But even apart from the Lord's immediate return, the Christian hope of joyous resurrection to eternal life seemed far superior to the notion of rebirth. These early Christians understood that death, the final enemy, had been conquered through the sacrificial death and victorious resurrection of Jesus of Nazareth and that the judgment of the wicked would be accomplished once and for all at the Great White Throne (Rev 20:11). Christians then as now looked forward to an existence in a new life with God for eternity, where worship, joy, knowledge and spiritual growth would be a permanent state of affairs. Jesus had said, *"I am the resurrection and the life; he who believes in me, though he die, yet shall he live, and whoever lives and believes in me shall never die"* (Jn 11:25-26). The Christian church fully understood this; hence the concept of reincarnation was as useful to them as a door in the bottom of a rowboat.

5
Past-Life Recall

ONE OF THE MOST SEEMINGLY convincing and enigmatic arguments for reincarnation is that of past-life recall. This phenomenon, as the name implies, is the ability of a person to recall details of an alleged "previous life." Basically, recall falls into two categories, *hypnotic regression* and *spontaneous recall*. The former is induced by hypnotic trance in which the hypnotist directs the subject with various suggestions. In most instances, the hypnotist is able to evoke in the subject some sort of "past-life" imagery. Spontaneous recall seems a bit more genuine simply because the "memories" are not provoked by an intermediary. These cases usually, but not always, occur in children, who insist that they are really someone else who has lived in the past. In both types of recall, some of the historical detail may prove to be true, and these incidents fuel the speculative fires of reincarnationists.

There are thousands of stories and accounts of various types of recall of supposed past lives. One example which is quite representative appeared in the July 1915 issue of

The American Magazine, and was entitled "Was It Reincarnation?" According to the story, the author's younger half
sister, Anne, exhibited a difference in both appearance and
behavior from the rest of the family. She was dark and
swarthy, looking more French or Spanish than the rest of
her lighter, Scotch-Irish family. As soon as she could talk,
Anne would identify with another lifetime and when repri-
manded for a bad habit would insist, "I've always done it
that way!"

One day her father probed her at length about her past
life. She insisted that she was formerly a soldier in Canada,
stating proudly, "I took the gates!" Her father asked what
her name was. "Lishus Faber," she answered. Impressed by
her behavior and insistence upon facts, her sister researched Canadian history books for a year trying to verify
the story. On the point of giving up, she was leafing through
a "funny old volume" that ended her search:

> It was a brief account of the taking of a little walled city
> by a small company of soldiers, a distinguished feat of
> some sort, yet of no general importance. A young lieu-
> tenant with his small band—the phrase leaped to my eyes
> —"took the gates" . . . and the name of the young lieu-
> tenant was Aloysius Le Febre![1]

The central problem with this and similar accounts revolves
around the fundamental question of the historicity of the
events and the veracity of the person relating them. And,
assuming (or even proving) the *facts* to be true, do recall
experiences necessarily validate reincarnation?

Of course, there is nothing quite so compelling as an idea
whose time has come. Therefore it is not surprising that
many psychics and hypnotherapists have turned their attention to reincarnation and recall phenomena. In 1977
Time magazine examined the trend:

> Ralph Grossi, a Pittsburgh hypnotherapist, travels to
> ten clinics in Pennsylvania, Ohio and West Virginia
> where he treats some 25 people a week with past-lives

therapy at $75 per session. An Arizona couple, Dick and Trenna Sutphen, who say they first met and married thousands of years ago, not only operate group seminars but also market tape recordings enabling patients to treat themselves at home. Typically Dick Sutphen hypnotizes 150 customers at a time; by unearthing the secrets of their past lives, he claims he helps them overcome depression, tension and sexual problems.[2]

The Sutphens have recently announced publication of a new monthly magazine, *Reincarnation Report,* which will be devoted entirely to the subject. The magazine "will feature the latest research and new directions in the field of past-life investigative therapy."[3] The editors claim to have contacted "over 600 regressive hypnotists, occult practitioners and researchers" to contribute to their magazine.

Two of the most important researchers in the area of past-life recall are Dr. Helen Wambach of San Francisco, who specializes in hypnotic regression, and Dr. Ian Stevenson of the University of Virginia, who gives primary attention to spontaneous recall and has been researching this area for over twenty years.

Helen Wambach

Although she has engaged in past-life research only about half as long as Stevenson, Dr. Helen Wambach has attained an equal amount of public and scientific attention. A licensed hypnotherapist, Wambach claimed to have hypnotically regressed over two thousand subjects at the time she wrote her book *Reliving Past Lives: The Evidence under Hypnosis* in 1978. Her technique is quite similar to other past-life hypnotists. She often does her therapy in groups. After soliciting volunteers (usually people with more than a passing interest in reincarnation), she puts them into a hypnotic trance. Once the subjects are "under," she asks them to "go back to 1750"—or 900 or some other arbitrary date—and "describe your impressions." Sometimes she gets no response, in which case she tries another date. The great majority of her subjects come up with remarkably detailed descriptions of life in some previous place and time.

In other instances, she uses the "world tour" technique: We're going to float back all around the world, back into past time. When I call out the name of a place, let the images come into your mind. An image for the Far East . . . an image for Central Asia . . . an image for Europe . . . an image for the Near East and Africa . . . or an image for North, Central or South America. . . . Now choose your character.[4]

Obviously there is considerable suggestive give-and-take between Wambach and her patients. She sometimes prods them with verbal questions to elicit more detail, which usually has positive results. Wambach once stated that up to eighty per cent of her subjects "telepathically anticipated my questions . . . so I purposely 'ask' some questions mentally."[5] In altered states of consciousness such as hypnosis, people seem to be susceptible to paranormal or telepathic communications from a variety of sources, including the spirit world or psychic realm, but the exact nature of the hypnotic state, including the sources of information which the subject recalls, is still very much an unsolved riddle.

Needless to say, such techniques do yield a volume of detail, some mundane, some semiarcane and some interesting; much of it is charted and catalogued in her book. How does she explain it? On the record Wambach is scientific and cautious, claiming that her research does not prove reincarnation. In one TV interview she simply said, "People are actually reproducing the past. I don't know how they're doing it."[6] On another occasion she speculated on the dynamics of the hypnotic state: "I think the brain is just like a receiver and it just tunes in on what 'is.' "[7]

Concerning her personal belief and practice, Wambach is quite open. In her book she describes her early parapsychology experiments with surprising naiveté and candor. She and a group of students attempted to contact the spirit world through "table tipping," a form of seance in which the participants sit around a table and summon the presence of unseen spirits, not unlike the Ouija board. She claims that an entity calling himself "Ethan" arrived and began to demonstrate his prowess by tipping the table. According to Wambach, he virtually possessed one of the group, a girl named Anna, and spoke through her in a male voice. Despite persistent interrogation, Ethan never revealed his true identity, preferring to wax eloquent on matters of occult and gnostic philosophy. Later, Ethan or some other entity apparently possessed Wambach herself, and she began to produce automatic writings, which are common among spirit mediums. In a trance, she wrote very complex mathematical formulas of which she claimed to have no prior knowledge, and she also produced the following cryptic rendition of gnostic theology: "The God concept is on its way out in the hierarchical sense... Jesus tried to alter this concept... by this he [Jesus] meant that we were all co-creators of the universe."[8]

While she explains her automatic writing as simply a natural phenomenon of tapping into some form of ethereal hidden knowledge, it is well known that automatic writing has long been associated with mediumship. Considering her admitted participation in seances in which she was the group leader, it is quite possible that Wambach is indeed a practicing medium—whether she knows it or not. Of course, this has deep implications for her work as a hypnotherapist. Having observed her firsthand as she lectured to a group of amateur parapsychologists and New Age spiritual dabblers, I can say that she is indeed a sympathizer with the growing movement of occultists, spiritists and psychics.[9] Aside from her spiritual allegiance, it should also be noted that she draws a considerable portion of her income from her vested interest in reincarnation. In 1977 she charged twenty dollars per person per session, and she has regressed some two thousand people; she is also paid lecture honorariums and book royalties.[10] While I do not intend to imply that she is financially unscrupulous, one can easily see that Wambach is not purely objective in her approach to the subject of reincarnation.

Various inconsistencies have appeared in her data and methods. While she claims that only 11 of 1,088 data sheets showed factual or historical discrepancies, she admits that she did not have the time and resources to trace many details. Another problem which she has not recognized concerns the dating procedure she uses with her subjects. For example, one of her clients claimed in a former life to have died in 2083 B.C.[11] Since the subject was in a trance telling the story as if she *were* that person, how could she use such wording? People who lived at that time had no knowledge that they were living "before Christ," nor did they have a dating system that would reflect this. Her subjects frequently use this "B.C." terminology.

Many hypnotherapists such as Wambach claim that the phobias and neuroses of this life can be resolved by finding their source in such a past life. For example, a fear of water could be traced to a drowning experience in a previous incarnation. But this does not prove the historical reality of such a life. Wambach, a trained psychologist, admits that "it is true that people release symptoms much faster with this kind of explanation they are providing for themselves. It is a pretty effective means of therapy, but *it doesn't prove reincarnation*" (emphasis mine).[12] In assessing Wambach's personal spiritual experiences and allegiance as well as her techniques, one must conclude that her research is far from scientific; it cannot substantiate a belief in the validity of reincarnation.

Ian Stevenson

Dr. Ian Stevenson is a careful and painstaking researcher, having flown many thousands of miles to all parts of the globe since 1960 in order to check out the facts and details of spontaneous recall cases. His reputation as an authority on reincarnation has spread swiftly; his files at the University of Virginia now contain over two thousand reports of alleged recall cases from around the world.

In the cases he deals with at length in his book *Twenty Cases Suggestive of Reincarnation,* all concern children ten years old or younger. Typically, the subject begins to manifest personality quirks as early as age two. These quirks soon develop into a pattern in which the child insists he or she is really someone else—someone who has lived and died in the surrounding area in the recent past. Stevenson, usually aided by interpreters, arrives on the scene and interviews the child, taking copious notes on all the details the subject remembers from the past life. Stevenson then checks these details with the family of the deceased person alleged to have been reincarnated.

Of those cases which Stevenson has researched in depth, he has found a remarkable degree of accuracy (about ninety per cent) in the data. The details are not general but quite specific, including names, locations, events and descriptions of households and family relations. In some cases the subject will insist that a certain object or previously owned item is kept in a location unknown to anyone else; upon checking, Stevenson finds the item and verifies the subject's knowledge of it.

Stevenson has carefully constructed his methods to allow for fraud and other cultural and coincidental influences. His work has been reviewed by other scientists, and none has faulted his scientific method. The technical publication *Journal of Nervous and Mental Disease,* highly respected in medical and scientific communities, devoted the majority of its September 1977 issue to Stevenson and his work. The serious consideration of reincarnation research by such a group of "hard scientists" underscores both Stevenson's reputation and the influence of rebirth speculation and psychic research in contemporary Western society.

Stevenson approaches his subject with a healthy skepticism. In laying the foundation for possible conclusions, he says that "the statements attributed to the subject are memories of some kind, and the question is whether they are memories of what he has heard or learned *normally,* or what he has experienced *paranormally,* or of what he has experienced in a previous life" (Stevenson's emphasis).[13]

The possibility that his subjects learn their information normally is certainly possible, although Stevenson doubts it because of the mass of paranormal evidence he has gathered. To decrease the possibility further, he discounts cases where the subject is an adult: "I'm suspect of cases in which the subject is an adult because you can't really control the subconscious influences derived from information to which the adult has been exposed."[14]

However, Ian Stevenson is, by his own admission, a parapsychologist, and all parapsychologists lean toward a paranormal or "spiritual" explanation for their work and findings. Stevenson himself does not divulge his personal spiritual belief and practice, and claims neither to believe nor disbelieve in reincarnation, although it is evident that he leans toward some form of rebirth as the best explanation for his findings.[15]

Stevenson compares the establishment of the possibility of reincarnation to the task a historian or a lawyer faces in proving facts. He points out that some cases are, in fact, "weak in both detail and authentication." Some cases "suggest reincarnation," others "furnish considerable evidence for it" and finally the "evidence can be persuasive even when not compelling."[16]

However, his analogy is not quite valid. Lawyers and historians have access to written records, photographs, objects and so on, which constitute empirical data much less subject to *interpretation* than spiritual or paranormal phenomena. Stevenson admits the strong possibility of spir-

itistic influence, whether by the "spirit" of the deceased
or even by demonic possession. And until humans know all
there is to know about the cosmic or heavenly worlds, reincarnation can hardly be proved via these methods. The
introduction of the possibility of spirit communication car-
ries with it the danger of spiritual deception. Since Stevenson seriously entertains the theory of demonic possession,
purposeful deception must be considered.

Dr. Stevenson's scientific skepticism is a healthy sign and
laudable trait, especially in an area with as many pitfalls
and sinkholes as psychic research. Nonetheless, several
problems still remain in his work: (1) The information he
relies on is not written down prior to attempts at verification. "A central difficulty in all such enquiries," acknowl-
edges Stevenson, "lies in the unreliability of the memories
(and even perceptions) of the experients and the witnesses."[17] (2) Recognitions of the people and places of the
alleged previous life are usually not observed by neutral
parties.[18] (3) There is an average gap of three to five years
between the first symptoms of previous existence and the
generation of publicity. (4) In the general cultural milieu of
all his examples there is a consensus regarding the validity
of reincarnation; the recall experiences that "check out"
are not uniformly scattered throughout the cultures of the
earth. As Stevenson says, "The incidence of reported cases
varies widely between different cultures. . . . [American
cases] are much weaker in details [and less frequent in
occurrence] than cases in Asia."[19]

Stevenson's scientific method and sane, cautious approach to his work undoubtedly must be considered an
important contribution in the growing area of psychic and
paranormal research. Yet, the *significance* of his contribution has to be determined by an *evaluation* and *definition*
of the things he has reported, not to mention the identity
and nature of the forces that produce the phenomena and
data. Fundamentally, this all boils down to the question of

spiritual discernment—the ability to determine whether paranormal phenomena are good, neutral or bad. A fundamental assumption of the Judeo-Christian world view is that there is a spiritual kingdom of darkness which has actively opposed the kingdom of God since the dawn of human history. The Prince of Darkness exerts his influence behind the scenes in many ways and on many levels of human endeavor; one of the principal methods of deceit is through the propagation of false religion and erroneous spiritual ideas. Hence, any body of data and persistent occurrence of phenomena which would tend to promote belief in reincarnation must be viewed with spiritual discernment.

Some further questions must be asked concerning the motives and presuppositions of the people who report these cases. (Remember that Stevenson has been deluged by such reports and has over two thousand of them on file.) The very fact that these cases are directed to a world-renowned *reincarnation researcher* is significant and indicates at least partial affirmation of the doctrine on the part of all involved. Are these people believers in rebirth theories before the cases are reported? How much subtle or overt reinforcement of the doctrine of reincarnation and the alleged reality of the "previous life" goes on in the months or years that elapse between the first symptoms and the arrival of Stevenson or other researchers? How does this affect the body of factual detail?

All these questions and objections need to be considered, for this type of research goes far beyond the realm of science, and real inquiries need to be made in the areas of philosophy and theology. One medical doctor summed up Stevenson's work in the *Journal of Nervous and Mental Disease* thus: "Either he is making a colossal mistake, or he will be known (I have said as much to him) as 'the Galileo of the 20th century.' "[20]

Problems with Past-Life Recall

Having detailed the work of Wambach and Stevenson, I want to offer some general critical observations about the subject of past-life recall. First is the problem of spurious or "faked" cases and faulty or misleading data. Most of the research and tales detailing past lives comes from people who are proreincarnation, and therefore the tendency is to promote or publicize the favorable cases and ignore the ones that don't check out.

One of the best-known cases is that of "Bridey Murphy," a Colorado housewife named Ruth Simmons who claimed to have lived previously in nineteenth-century Ireland. While some reincarnationists still cite the Murphy case as evidence, occult authority Walter Martin, president of Christian Research Institute in San Juan Capistrano, California, has shown that "Bridey" picked up all her knowledge both consciously and subconsciously from her Irish nanny. Renee Haynes, editor of the British Society for Psychical Research's *Journal of Proceedings,* concurs with Martin and concludes that Bridey Murphy has been debunked and laid to rest.[21]

Another debatable case is that of Edward Ryall, an Englishman who describes his former life in seventeenth-century England in his book *Second Time Round.* Stevenson directed considerable attention to the Ryall case and felt that Ryall's claims were so accurate in detail that he could command the respect of historians of Restoration England. Haynes, however, has also looked into this case and says that Ryall's book

has much in common with Blackmore's *Lorna Doone* and Conan Doyle's *Micah Clark,* as well as containing various snippets of anachronistic archaism . . . and exhibiting an almost total incomprehension of the assumptions, manners, customs and cookery of the period. Recent investigations, moreover, have shown that the well preserved local church registers do not mention his "remembered" name, and that the site of the farmhouse in which he claims to have lived was unreclaimed common land until after the Enclosure Acts.[22]

Where to draw the line between outright fakery and some sort of inadvertent or subconscious manipulation of spurious facts and details is hard to determine. Many people subjected to hypnotic regression come up with details that are hidden or stored deep in their minds. For example, it is generally believed that most or all sensory impressions, including facts assimilated through reading, conversation and so on, are permanently stored in the brain's molecular "memory bank." The great majority of this information is suppressed in normal consciousness, but in an altered state, especially hypnosis, the brain is able to recall these details. This phenomenon is referred to as "cryptoamnesia." Cryptoamnesia undoubtedly accounts for many of the minuscule historical details which come to light during spontaneous recall or hypnotic regressions into alleged past lives. A good example is given by Harold Rosen in his book *A Scientific Report on the Search for Bridey Murphy:*

For example, under hypnosis one man began speaking in Oscan, a language spoken in Italy in the third century B.C. He was even able to write down an Oscan curse. Only later, during additional sessions of hypnosis, was it discovered that the man had recently looked at an Oscan grammar in the library. Several phrases had registered in his unconscious mind and found expression in the hypnotic state.[23]

Another fabrication was exposed by English Jesuit Joseph Crehan. He had dealt with a woman who claimed a previous existence as a seventh-century Jesuit. Crehan had access to Jesuit records of the period but could find no evidence at all of such a person having existed.[24]

It is noteworthy that these discrepancies are usually pointed out by people with no vested interest in reincarnation. Those writers who are favorable to rebirth theories usually avoid mention of examples which might challenge their beliefs.

A second problem surrounding past-life recall is that of contradictory findings by researchers. Conclusions of the more thorough researchers sometimes clash; for example, Wambach claims that the races are intermingled from life to life, whereas Stevenson's research tends to negate this. In all of Stevenson's twenty cases the subjects were allegedly reborn in their same ethnic group. The span between incarnations is also divergent. Wambach says about fifty-one years pass between births, while Stevenson reports five to ten years. Geddes MacGregor takes a rather dim view of recall as a proof of reincarnation, pointing out that many cases have proven bogus. He comments, "The literature on this subject is considerable; the results, though they leave many unresolved puzzles, are inconclusive."[25]

All in all, if this type of research is to be accepted as scientifically valid, the methods and data of researchers will have to be compared and cross-referenced. Furthermore, more attention should be given to the percentage of faked, debunked and spurious cases and those with questionable or faulty data. A third consideration concerns the *motivations* and *personal spiritual beliefs* of the researchers themselves, which need to be clearly stated. All scientific and historical work is undertaken with certain "agendas" or assumptions. In an area as highly charged as reincarnation, they need to be forthrightly spelled out.

A fourth problem with recall findings centers on the very nature of hypnotic regression. Stevenson, who does not deal with hypnotically regressed subjects, tells why:

> The "personalities" usually evoked during hypnotically induced regressions to a "previous life" seem to comprise a mixture of several ingredients. These may include the subject's current personality, his expectations of what he thinks the hypnotist wants, his fantasies of what he thinks his previous life ought to have been, and

also perhaps elements derived paranormally.[26]

J. B. Rhine of Duke University, often called "the father of American Parapsychology," commenting on Bridey Murphy, says there is no way of knowing whether Ruth Simmons did not already have the facts stored in her mind via cryptoamnesia, and then raises the possibility of extrasensory perception (ESP) as a source for her knowledge:

> It is also possible that this young woman could have gained her knowledge through telepathy or clairvoyance, two forms we call extrasensory perception (ESP). ... [Also] for a careful study of so important a matter as reincarnation, it would be necessary to know what went on in the conversations that took place with the girl awake, between sessions, as well as when hypnotized.[27]

A fifth and final consideration when dealing with recall phenomena is that of cultural and religious conditioning. This is especially relevant in spontaneous recall cases. What is the spiritual or religious background of the subject? Since most subjects are children, what are the beliefs and practices of the parents and how might these influences be exerted? This question is particularly important when dealing with any type of psychic manifestations. Occultists frequently have psychic experiences dating to early childhood, particularly if the parents are adherents of some form of occult belief and practice.

In every case of Stevenson's study, the subjects were surrounded by a cultural and religious milieu that encouraged belief in reincarnation. Stevenson spent considerable time researching spontaneous recall among the Tlingit Indians of Alaska, who have a highly developed belief in reincarnation. Consequently Alaska has the highest percentage of recall cases in the United States, according to Stevenson. The Druses of the Mideast believe in *immediate* reincarnation, in which the soul of the deceased is immediately reborn. While researching a case of spontaneous recall there

Stevenson observed, "We should therefore feel no surprise that the incidence of cases among the Druses is perhaps the highest in the world."[28]

However, in Western culture Stevenson has found a much different pattern. In 1978 he remarked that

[American cases] are much weaker in details than those in non-Western countries, such as Asia. American children who say they remember previous lives rarely recall many details that would permit verification. When they do remember some verifiable details, they are usually those in the life of another member of the family.[29]

In light of these difficulties many psychologists are cautious or skeptical in assessing past-life recall. *Time* concluded its article with some salient observations of the whole scene with this trenchant note and a quotation from Alexander Rogawski, former chief of the Los Angeles County Medical Association's psychiatry section:

Indeed, the past-lives movement is cashing in on the disillusionment with conventional therapies, fear of death and the current interest in the occult. "But all that the therapy's popularity proves," says Rogawski, is that "suckers are born every minute and customers can be found for everything."[30]

Dr. Lucille Forer, member of the board of directors of the Los Angeles County Psychological Association, said that most of her contemporaries were skeptical about regression therapy:

A good therapist may be able to use any material brought up from a patient's subconcious, but if a person believed past lives were actually being tapped, it could lead to disturbed feelings. A person could develop psychosis if the fantasy material was extreme. He could feel guilt about what he thought were past acts. I would warn anyone who wants to do this sort of thing to do it with a trained person who can handle any problems that might arise. Just as with the body therapies of the 1970s, people are

looking for shortcuts that don't exist.[31]
Whatever the case, there is some kind of experiential reality behind many past-life recalls. Rather than write them all off as products of overactive imaginations or contrived and jury-rigged accounts, it may prove fruitful to delve deeper into this phenomenon in order to make some sense of it, as chapter six attempts to do.

6

Sorting It Out: Possible Explanations of Past-Life Recall

IT IS SAID THAT BUDDHA ISSUED detailed instructions on how to recall previous lives, so the phenomenon is hardly new. We can assume that his disciples had reasonably good success in conjuring up past existences, judging from the doctrine's acceptance in contemporary Buddhism. Exactly what techniques Buddha prescribed is uncertain, but it is doubtful that they differed much from the current mélange of psychospiritual methods. In any case, people do recall *something* in the pursuit of past lives—but what is the source of these experiences?

Natural Explanations
Natural explanations of recall phenomena might also fall under the rubric of psychology. Here it is useful to turn again to Helen Wambach, who, despite her shortcomings as a scientist, honestly confronts some natural explanations for reincarnation memories. In her book she states,

> We are told that we use 10% of our brain. I have come to believe that those portions of the brain that we think

of as having no specific function—the remaining 90%
—are indeed operating constantly.... Does our subconscious create past-life impressions from the scraps of our
current life, *in the way it creates our dreams?* Or do these
reincarnation memories under hypnosis reflect the real
past? (emphasis mine)[1]

A California newspaper reporter had similar questions
after she interviewed Wambach: "Wambach couldn't ignore ... the sophistication of her subjects. All were aware
that the hypnosis sessions were intended to reveal their
past lives. And Wambach could not vouch for their knowledge of history, or lack of it."[2]

It seems that Wambach answers her own rhetorical questions in describing her techniques. After telling her subjects to regress into a past life and giving them a date and
place, she says things like this: "Now the spirit is leaving
the body. Allow yourself to experience the spirit leaving
the body. What are you experiencing now?" She says, "So
I would include in my hypnotic technique instructions to
touch, to hear sounds, to taste, to smell, or to have emo-
tions."[3]

Many authorities feel that natural explanations are more
than adequate, particularly for explaining hypnotic regressions. Renee Haynes believes that the strong directives become self-fulfilling: "It follows that when a person is told
to remember previous lives, he will automatically accept the
implicit suggestion that he did indeed have such lives; an
acceptance made the more complete because he is telepathically aware of the hypnotist's conviction that it is so."[4]

Professor Ernest Hilgard, director of the Hypnosis Research Laboratory at Stanford University, considers all
claims of past-life regression to be nonsense:

Hypnosis is a very dangerous tool best used by formally
trained people. New identities claimed during trance
are not uncommon and very easy to produce. Invariably,
they're related to long buried memories, and anybody

who makes claims to the contrary has not based them on scholarly judgments.[5]

Several experts quoted in *Time* magazine echoed similar opinions skeptical of hypnotic regression:

British Psychiatrist Anthony Storr argues that recall of past lives is really an example of cryptoamnesia, a fantasy based upon subconscious recollections of some long-forgotten historical novel or magazine article. Says Storr: "Most us us have a B movie running in our heads most of the time." Alexander Rogawski, former chief of the Los Angeles County Medical Association's psychiatry section, is even less kind to past-lives treatment: "It's a mystic takeoff on psychoanalysis... one of those fads that come and go like mushrooms."[6]

The *National Enquirer* provides an example of the extremes to which hypnotic recall can be put.[7] Several years ago, they reported on the work of one California "hypnologist," Dr. John Kappas, who "progressed" actor Robert Cummings one hundred years into the future, where he gave vivid details of his "next" life. (If you can go back to your past, why not go forward?) Speaking in a hoarse mutter under hypnosis, Cummings claimed that he was/will be born in 1989 in Canton, China, where he becomes a doctor. He claims the average lifespan is 150 years in the year 2079, and humanity has solved many of its problems.

Indeed, the entire episode as described is identical to hypnotic regressions of past lives in both detail and results, raising yet more vexing questions about the nature of hypnosis. Whatever the case, people are presently being conditioned on both subtle and overt levels to accept the possibility of reincarnation. The bombardment from the media definitely heightens the expectations of many people, who are thus more likely to interpret their dreams, déjà vu and hypnotic experiences as evidences of former lives.

Psychic Explanations

Natural explanations probably account for the bulk of regression experiences. But we cannot brush aside the substantial percentage of verified cases that cannot be explained naturally, where intersecting data has raised serious questions which indicate the factuality of the events recalled. Ian Stevenson feels strongly that there must be a paranormal, or psychic explanation (which to him includes the possibility of genuine reincarnation), behind many documented cases of spontaneous recall.

This, of course, brings up the question of the nature and reality of psychic phenomena. Science has recently been trying to quantify and prove the reality of existence beyond our five senses, and so the terms *psychic* and *psychic phenomena* have been applied to things that people in past times have always called "spiritual." These include such paranormal occurrences as extrasensory perception (ESP), clairvoyance and telepathic communication. The existence of psychic phenomena has now been well documented, and most people believe in the reality of the spiritual/psychic world in one form or another. Assuming its validity, we should view some reincarnation experiences and evidence in this context—but with caution, discernment and objective skepticism.

Although rationalism with its scientific skepticism has been a powerful force in recent history, its influence is beginning to wane, and people are turning again to look for spiritual answers to life's meaning, as they have throughout history. And, while natural explanations for reincarnation phenomena are valid, they do not answer all the questions that are raised. The existence of paranormal phenomena is not in conflict with the Christian world view. In fact, biblically speaking, one cannot deny the reality of spiritual powers. The essentially spiritual nature of humanity and the reality of the afterlife, to say nothing of angels and demons, are central to a Christian understanding of human life and the struggle of good and evil. After all, is not God himself "supernatural"? The Bible assumes the existence of disembodied spirit creatures, both good and bad; however, it also teaches that the evil ones seek to deceive us. The teachings of Jesus in the Gospels on this subject leave little doubt that supernatural agencies are at work "behind the scenes," acting strategically to influence events. What are the ramifications of such spiritual warfare for regression phenomena and past-lives experiences?

Spiritism and Reincarnation

One of the more obvious explanations of genuinely paranormal cases of reincarnation recall would seem to be *direct spirit influence,* as the great majority of cases exhibit features parallel with those of spiritism, seances, mediumship and demonic possession.

Stevenson says that if information about a past life could be proved to come from spirit communication, it would cause serious problems: "Such a case, if we find one, would severely shake confidence in the subjective experience of memory."[8] It would also disturb reincarnation theories based on past-life recall. Stevenson agrees nonetheless that "the influence of some discarnate personality" is indeed an option, along with telepathy and clairvoyance. He even admits that mediums can duplicate the feats of detailed recall, saying, "Perhaps the children who remember previous lives really add to this number."[9] While he himself leans toward reincarnation as the genuine meaning of past-life recall, he notes that many features of the cases "do not permit a firm decision between the hypothesis of possession and reincarnation."[10] He does state that a "significant minority" of his subjects exhibited ESP or mediumistic tendencies.

Regression therapist Edith Fiore, who has a long waiting list of clients, makes a similar observation. "Sometimes multiple personalities emerge under hypnosis. Sometimes they're nonintegrated past life personalities and sometimes they're from a splitting up of the personality of this life. *They could also be entities of some sort*" (emphasis mine).[11]

Wambach, too, tells of encounters with spirits in her early hypnosis experiences: "I knew that many people active in the occult field felt that demonic possession was a danger when people were hypnotized.... I was now to enter a bypass [sic]. As ghosts and spirits, seances, strange messages and automatic writing began to appear, I learned far more than I ever anticipated."[12]

Connection with Spirits

A good example of what may be called "the spirit connection" is the well-known novelist Taylor Caldwell, author of *Great Lion of God* and *Dear and Glorious Physician* among others. While under hypnosis, she allegedly recalled over a dozen previous lives, including that of Mary Magdalene's mother, through whom she claims to have met Jesus. She drew on a reservoir of psychic abilities in order to reproduce the historical details in her novels; as one observer said, "The information just poured out of her."[13] Not surprisingly, the generator behind all this psychic voltage was a spirit which was innocuously dubbed "The Presence":

> Without her specifically saying so, I knew she often wondered how some of the material for her books had formed in her typewriter.... She felt at times an overwhelming link with a universe full of shadowy personalities. A nameless Presence, to whom she hesitated to give a name, was sensed at times even by her husband, a very practical man. This hovering Presence had the eeriness of another life, and another planet, and its largeness seemed to fill the room. And yet she could neither see nor touch it. She could only sense it. The Presence came and went unexpectedly.[14]

Stevenson tells about an interesting case of actual possession, although he inexplicably treats it as a case of reincarnation. In the spring of 1954 an Indian boy named Jasbir, aged three and a half, took ill with smallpox and then lapsed into a coma which his family temporarily mistook for death. A few hours later he stirred and finally revived. Upon regaining his faculties several weeks later, he displayed a remarkable transformation of behavior, claiming to be a Brahmin named Sobha Ram, who had died in an accident at the age of twenty-two on May 22, 1954. This case displayed all the normal features of Stevenson's subjects except that it clearly was not a case of reincarnation, since Jasbir was three-and-a-half years old at the time of Sobha Ram's death. Instead, we seem to have a clear case of possession—either by the discarnate personality of Sobha Ram, or by a spirit or demon impersonating him.

This was confirmed by "the voice of Sobha Ram" speaking through Jasbir. "Mr. Ram" stated rather matter-of-factly that after death he had met a *sadhu* (holy man) who told him to "take cover" in Jasbir's body.[15] Complicating matters, Jasbir's family said that the time of his illness was in April or May of 1954: Ram died late in May. So the time of initial possession may well have taken place *before* Sobha Ram's death. If so, and it seems likely, this only increases the probability of spirit possession. Stevenson says that the facts of this case do constitute an "unusual feature," but he never pursues the persistent hard questions that are raised: First, it cannot be considered a case of classical reincarnation because Jasbir had his own personality prior to the possession. Any parent will attest that three-and-a-half-year-olds *do* have personalities. Second, Jasbir and Sobha Ram lived in nearby villages during the three-and-one-half-year period from 1950 to 1954. Third, two "souls" were inhabiting one body, contrary to what the doctrine of reincarnation teaches. Yet in every other respect this case has exact parallels with the examples that Stevenson treats as reincarnation: Jasbir, for example, was able to recall many details of Sobha Ram's life. It seems that there has been a miscue here by someone or something; in theatrical parlance, "the mask has slipped."

In his general discussion at the back of his book, Stevenson relates a similar story with darkly humorous overtones:

Some of the [spirit] communicators addressing Wickland [a spiritualist author] through the mediumship of his wife asserted that they had erroneously "possessed" an incarnate personality's body in the mistaken idea that they could reincarnate. When they discovered their error, they apologized and withdrew.[16]

How do they do it? Two of the big questions concerning mediumship and demonic possession revolve around what may be called "spiritual technology": How do spirits gain access to the great wealth of mundane details about a person, and how are they able to "possess" a person so as to take over all of that person's functions?

Sir John Eccles once said that "the brain is a machine that a ghost can operate." Perhaps this nonchalant one-liner is close to the truth. Mediums and occultists who are taken over or possessed by a spirit generally do it by entering a deep trance and relinquishing control over the mind and body. Thus, in the absence of the human spirit, no one is at the controls, and a discarnate spirit can conceivably slide in and take over.

Paul Twitchell, a medium and eclectic occultist who founded *Eckankar*, "The Ancient Science of Soul Travel," details this "technology" in one of his esoteric writings. He describes two techniques used by spirits in mediumship:

They are the trance, in which the communicator uses the mind by shutting off the thoughts and making it blank. It [the spirit] then takes advantage of this condition and uses it as a vehicle to pass the message on to the audience. ... The other method is often known as mind-to-mind contact, a state in which the entity [spirit] uses its power and force to inject ideas into the medium's mind with the medium's own consciousness being withdrawn.[17]

To explain the great number of details that spirit beings

seem able to know, several options are possible. One is that spirits, having been presumably living and active for thousands of years, have accumulated a great deal of information, whether by observation or through accumulation in some sort of spiritual "data bank." The biblical concept of *familiar spirits* derives from this familiarity with a particular family, cultural/ethnic group or geographical area. Edmond Gruss in his booklet on the Ouija board offers some further insight:

> One J. Raupert gives this account: "Some years ago I had a striking experience of this kind, the spirit for many months claiming to be a deceased friend of mine and furnishing many remarkable proofs of his identity. Upon being discovered in a manifest contradiction and falsehood, however, and charged in the name of God to reveal the true source of his information, he declared that he got it all out of our silly 'thought boxes,' it being possible for him to read the contents of the passive mind with the same ease with which we read a book or newspaper."[18]

While any such "spirit confession" must be as suspect as its source, the basic technique described here seems plausible and correlates with other spiritualist lore. Another theory holds that spirits are able to affect the physical realm through manipulation of the electromagnetic spectrum. Since the human brain and nervous system operate on electrical impulses, it is conceivable that a spirit might read our mental broadcasts or transmit its own into the human mind.

Not all psychic explanations necessarily involve demonic spirit beings. In his general discussion Stevenson mentions two similar historical examples which have parallels with the Jasbir-Sobha Ram case. In one, an engraver named Thompson suddenly felt compelled to paint certain scenes which arose vividly in his mind. Although he had little interest or skill in painting, Thompson turned out paint-

ings identical to those of a local painter named Gifford, who
had died six months before. Stevenson speculates that
Thompson had apparently fallen under the influence of
the "discarnate personality" of Gifford. Thompson writes,
"During the time I was sketching, I remember having the
impression that I was Mr. Gifford himself, and I would tell
my wife before starting out that Mr. Gifford wanted to go
sketching, although I did not know at that time that he had
died early in the year." In the second example, similar
manifestations occur:

> The case of Lurancy Vennum suggests a more complete
> possession. In this case, for several months (and occa-
> sionally afterwards) the personality of "Mary Roff" [who
> died when Lurancy Vennum was a year old] entirely dis-
> placed that of Lurancy Vennum and apparently occu-
> pied the vacated body of that girl. At the end of several
> months, "Mary Roff" departed and Lurancy Vennum
> resumed control. During her tenancy of the body, if we
> may call her manifestation such, "Mary Roff" never
> claimed to be Lurancy Vennum. She merely claimed to
> be herself, i.e., Mary Roff, occupying the temporarily
> available body of Lurancy Vennum.[19]

Whatever truthfulness these cases may or may not have,
there seems to be a shadowy nether world of overlapping
personality manifestations common both to mediums in
seances and to reincarnation experiences. Stevenson says
it is hard to draw the line: "Some sensitives or mediums
also experience a kind of identification with the persons
living or deceased about whom they received information.
They may use the first person in describing the experiences
of the person cognized."[20]

A surprising parallel to this syndrome pops up in an
unlikely place—in flying saucer lore. Many UFO investi-
gators have concluded that there is a definite tie-in between
UFO appearances, "close encounters of the third kind"
(occupant sightings), and run-of-the-mill spiritism and

occultism. John Keel, one of the world's best-known and respected UFO researchers reports that "in many modern UFO contact cases, the visible and apparently physical entities nearly always establish at the outset their complete knowledge of the contactee's past, often coming up with information about distant relatives unknown to the contactee which, when checked out, proves to be valid."[21]

In summarizing this discussion of the psychic and spiritistic parallels with past-life phenomena, several things should be noted. First, the relatively few examples of apparently genuine spontaneous recall cases can hardly be taken as proof of the doctrine of reincarnation. Of the logical interpretations remaining, it would seem that these cases resemble psychism, mediumship and spirit possession more closely than they do genuine rebirth. The biblical portrayal of familiar spirits or demonic possession seems more likely than actual reincarnation. But even without a biblical or Christian bias, parapsychologists should admit that the recall phenomenon, *when it cannot be explained by natural means,* is most correctly interpreted in the context of (1) extrasensory perception and clairvoyance; or (2) mediumship, trance communications or spirit possession.

Summing Up

As we have seen, authenticated recall phenomena can be understood by a variety of overlapping explanations. Three observations need to be made at this point. First, in those cases where hypnosis is used, it must be noted that hypnosis is not a purely neutral state and that the patient is highly susceptible to suggestions and other mental or psycho-spiritual transmissions. The nature and mechanism of the hypnotic state is still largely unknown. Second, the information gathered through ESP and other paranormal means is highly subjective, elusive and generally unreliable. Much of it is patently bogus and imaginary. For example, some eight hundred books and articles have been written on the recently publicized "life after death" research, regaling the public with an endless variety of psychic impressions, out-of-body experiences and beatific visions of celestial beings and spheres. Yet much of this alleged revelation is conflicting and confused, if not rather absurd, typifying the haphazardness of ESP. Third, recall experiences—especially those documented cases of spontaneous recall, which are the most reliable—are not at all common. Yet for those few that do exhibit seemingly genuine features of a supposed past life, we may consider a number of explanations that might account for the phenomenon.

1. *Conscious or unconscious fraud.* Fraud must be regarded as a strong possibility, especially in hypnotic regressions and in cases where the data is presented by proponents of reincarnation. It is not necessary to allege conscious bad intent in every instance, for there may be a strong element of subconscious motivation when proreincarnation people are dealing with the possibility of rebirth. And, it should be remembered, most if not all reincarnation researchers and hypnotherapists make their living through their research and practice, a fact which can affect their findings whether consciously or not.

2. *Cryptoamnesia.* A well-documented occurrence, cryptoamnesia most likely accounts for a large percentage of recall cases, both hypnotic and spontaneous. In fact, it is probably the most common source of past-life recall experiences. The case of Bridey Murphy discussed in chapter five is a good example.

3. *Genetic memory.* Some people hold that certain memories or characteristics of ancestry may be stored in our chromosome and DNA structure; each person is a combination of all the ancestors who have preceded him. In some ways such a theory seems reasonable and scientific, as the basic mechanism (the genetic structure) is known. But science has yet to document such a link in any way that would explain past-life recall.

4. *Spirit communication.* In speaking of spirit communication, we are dealing with two types of "spirits": the spirits of dead persons and those spirits that were never human, that is, demonic (or angelic) spirits. The Bible has much to say about demonic possession, but it says little about communication with the dead. However, it is clearly prohibited, as King Saul well knew. Wanting the dead Samuel's advice, he sought a medium to contact Samuel's spirit; and Saul *did* talk with the dead man (1 Sam 28:7-19). The possibility, though forbidden, is similarly implied in Isaiah 8:19: "And when they say to you, 'Consult the mediums and the wizards who chirp and mutter,' should not a people consult their God? Should they consult the dead on behalf of the living?" It is possible that the souls of the unredeemed may linger in some twilight zone, a zone where deception and struggle continue, such as C. S. Lewis describes in *The Great Divorce.* The question for Christians is not so much whether communication with the dead is possible as whether it is right. And the possibility remains that some recall instances may have put the receptive subject unintentionally in touch with the spirit of a dead person.

An even more sinister possibility is that a recall experience may have put the subject into contact with spiritual beings that never held human form. And, as Christianity holds, many of these spirits are demonic; that is, they are fallen beings whose intent is to deceive or harm. Distasteful as this possibility is, it must be considered as one explanation of recall phenomena. The methods and expressions of recall experiences and spiritistic experiences are very similar. Parallels between the utterances of mediums in seances and the trancelike statements of recall subjects are notable.

5. *The "collective unconscious."* Swiss psychologist Carl Jung has postulated a theory of the "collective unconscious" of the human race, an ethereal pool in which the thoughts, impressions and experiences of all humans mingle. His

theory is not unlike the occult theory of the akashic records; the *akasha* are said to be a vast cosmic data bank of information, containing impressions (or cosmic "videotapes") of all lives and events that have occurred. If there is any truth in such a theory, then the possibility would exist that a person in an altered state of consciousness could have access to this treasure-trove of information. As Illinois psychotherapist Lyn Tinsley has observed,

> I don't know that [recall] means the theory of reincarnation is true. The phenomenon may be retrocognition, a process whereby individuals have knowledge of events that occurred in the past. They may tap into something in the air. It's like precognition where people have images of a future event. It's the same thing only it's in the past.[22]

Jung's thought has been used as a springboard by Morton Kelsey, an Anglican clergyman and former professor of psychology at Notre Dame. Kelsey, who has written a number of books on the supernatural, postulates a "psychoid realm" which is similar to the theory of the akashic records. He feels that this is a much more likely explanation for past-life recall, stating that

> the idea of participation in a spiritual or psychoid realm is a simpler theory than reincarnation, and it explains more phenomena. In that non-physical world, events and people both continue to exist in a real sense. One can be in touch with any element from any time or place in this realm that sometimes seems like a vast bank of non-physical data.[23]

While Kelsey's views, as well as the theory of the akasha, may have dubious biblical warrant, they are at least options which merit some consideration. It has been said half facetiously that "there are more things in heaven than on earth." There is no good reason to doubt this, and the only question that remains unanswered is where the boundary lies.

7

World Views in Conflict: The Arguments for and against Reincarnation

MANY REINCARNATIONISTS insist that the repetitive patterns found in nature are valid evidence for rebirth cycles. Such cycles as the return of the seasons, the monthly cycle, the daily sunrise and the redistribution of water through evaporation and rain all are said to be macrocosmic examples of the destiny of each soul. The Bible, too, speaks of these things. Three thousand years ago Solomon sighed,

A generation goes, and a generation comes,
  but the earth remains for ever.
The sun rises and the sun goes down,
  and hastens to the place where it rises.
The wind blows to the south,
  and goes round to the north;
round and round goes the wind,
  and on its circuits the wind returns.
All streams run to the sea,
  but the sea is not full;
to the place where the streams flow,
  there they flow again. (Eccles 1:4-7)

Without doubt nature has its cycles, but does this prove
reincarnation? Life and death patterns are the same for
all living things, whether they be amoebas, trees, chip-
munks or people. And in all species the scenario is exactly
the same: a living thing is born, it reproduces, and then
dies. No one has ever seriously entertained the notion
that a chipmunk living in Wisconsin in 1982 might be a
reincarnation of a chipmunk that died in Minnesota in
1975. Is the stately elm that crowns our back yard a reincarnation of a wispy weeping willow that was cut down last
century? Such speculation is rather far-fetched. Chip-
munks, elms and humans all *reproduce*. This no one doubts.
But to insist that reproduction is somehow synonymous
with reincarnation is a quantum leap in logic too broad
to span.

Reincarnationists, however, believe that the strongest
arguments for their doctrines are neither nature's cycles
nor the evidences of past-life recall. Rather, they believe
that their most persuasive argument is a moral one. They
contend that only through the law of karma can true justice
be rendered, that only by experiencing many lifetimes is
a person able to get a fair shake. They insist that one life
is not enough for moral, intellectual and spiritual growth;
to them the Christian view of only one life followed by
judgment seems bigoted and narrow. As S. L. Cranston
puts it,

> For God or nature to allow human beings but one so-
> journ on earth, that has been evolving for millions of
> years and that affords almost illimitable opportunities
> for growth of intelligence, talents and moral powers,
> seems an inexcusable waste of human resources.[1]

Sri Chinmoy, an Indian guru who conducts regular meditation sessions at the United Nations in New York, expresses
similar sentiments: "Now if our aim is to enter into the
Highest, the Infinite, the Eternal, the Immortal, then naturally one short span of life is not enough."[2]

Only One Life?

This sentiment is usually aimed at biblical Christianity, either directly or indirectly. But thinking of reincarnation as "a great adventure" is a questionable notion in view of the perilous human condition as it is portrayed in the Bible and witnessed throughout world history. Life on our planet is not just sweetness and light; it is not a string of marvelous and fulfilling experiences. The element of moral evil which is all but dominant in our world cannot be ignored simply by appealing to "enlightenment" and "growth." Scripture teaches us with a stern consistency that God is deeply and passionately concerned about sin and evil—so much so that he became incarnate and died *in our place* and *for our sins* in the person of Jesus Christ, forgiving in an instant all the "bad karma" of those who believe and trust him. The forgiveness of God in the face of Jesus Christ is by any argument better than sheer justice; who would not rather choose mercy than the inescapable retribution of karma? Justice, fairness and love are more perfectly manifested in the divine act of reconciliation and forgiveness than through unremitting judgment and punishment.

Second, Christianity disagrees with the Eastern assumption that one lifetime is too short a time to develop a functional relationship between God and a person. This life does contain sufficient opportunities to grow morally. Responsibility cannot be evaded while one procrastinates until the next life.

Moral evolution, or growth, is not so much a *process* as it is a *choice*—a choice to love God and others and to do what is morally right. As Lao-tse said, "The journey of a thousand miles begins with the first step." (And, of course, the choice and intent to take that step.) Such a moral choice is not a matter of hundreds or thousands of lifetimes of tiny moral steps made in the distant hope that we will eventually learn our lessons and finally balance our karma. Instead, it is a choice anyone can (and must!) make each day. Ultimately, for the Christian, it is the awareness that we can never evolve to goodness on our own; instead we choose forgiveness, redemption and Christ's life in us. As the apostle Paul says, "Behold, *now* is the acceptable time; behold, *now* is the day of salvation" (2 Cor 6:2). And, for those who have made the choice, the promise rings eternal: "Blessed are those whose iniquities are forgiven, and whose sins are covered; blessed is the man against whom the Lord will not reckon his sin" (Rom 4:7-8).

Repentance, humility, self-sacrifice and compassion are characteristics any person can develop over the period of a lifetime with the help of God. Of course, our response to God is pivotal; as Geddes MacGregor says, "God does not promise to cause me to grow without my growing. He promises only the conditions for success."[3] Those conditions are the love, mercy and justice of God, applied to the Christian's life through the work of the Holy Spirit; but the initial step of conversion and forgiveness occurs in the span of time it takes to make a choice.

Is Heaven a Bore?
One misconception put forth by reincarnationists and shared by many people is that heaven is a rather boring place of obligatory hymn-singing, harp-playing and doing holy chores. This description is rather naive, as C. S. Lewis comments in *Christian Behavior:* "There is no need to be worried by facetious people who try to make the Christian hope of heaven ridiculous by saying that they don't want to 'spend eternity playing harps.' The answer to such people is that if they cannot understand books written for grown-ups, they should not talk about them."

Such misconceptions are perplexing, as they fail to take God's nature into account. If God were boring, then we might have some justifiable fears that heaven might become tedious or even tyrannical, but to seriously entertain such a notion is simply absurd. There is sufficient evidence from the created universe alone that God is infinite in his glory, creativity and power. Carl Henry ends the fourth volume of his massive theological commentary with these words: "There, face to face, our heavenly Father will unveil intimacies of love and knowledge hitherto unknown, and reserved for those who love him."[4] The apostle Paul also rejoiced in this hope nineteen hundred years ago, as reflected in some of his New Testament writings:

I consider that the sufferings of this present time are not worth comparing with the glory that is to be revealed to us. (Rom 8:18)

No eye has seen, nor ear heard, nor the heart of man conceived, what God has prepared for those who love him. (1 Cor 2:9)

And we all, with unveiled face, beholding the glory of the Lord, are being changed into his likeness from one degree of glory to another; for this comes from the Lord who is the Spirit. (2 Cor 3:18)

Even MacGregor, with his reincarnationist sympathies, says that "surely heaven must be an ongoing fulfillment . . . never be it said to have reached the point where no more development can take place."[5] Michael Paternoster elaborates:

Whereas I am indeed conscious of needing more than one lifetime to achieve the highest of which I am capable, I am more likely to achieve it by travelling on into another world than by a series of finite, self-contained and mutually exclusive lives. Indeed, I do not see heaven itself as static, precluding further progress. Surely, even the blessed can still advance "from glory to glory" as one will never know all that there is to know about the infinite God in whose society we may spend eternity.[6]

Justice and Judgment

Reincarnationists frequently object to the biblical theme of judgment and to the teaching that the ungodly and the wicked will be banned from the kingdom of God, insisting that a loving God could do no such thing. But would a God who did not react against evil be morally perfect? Would such a God be truly good? Imagine a society where laws are not enforced. Thievery, murder, rape and violence would go unpunished; society would break down into anarchy. Survival of the fittest would be the only recourse, and the weak and helpless would suffer continually at the hands of the strong, the cunning and the ruthless.

Only God's judgment provides us with an ultimate sense of justice. Leon Morris summarizes this well in his book *The Biblical Doctrine of Judgment:*

> The doctrine of final judgment... stresses man's accountability and the certainty that justice will finally triumph over all the wrongs which are part and parcel of life here and now.... The Christian view of judgment means that history moves to a goal. Judgment protects the idea of the triumph of God and of good. It is unthinkable that the present conflict between good and evil should last throughout eternity. Judgment means that evil will be disposed of authoritatively, decisively, finally. Judgment means that in the end God's will will be perfectly done.[7]

The biblical truths of judgment and condemnation of the wicked must be considered forthrightly, for they are consistent themes throughout Scripture. The Bible teaches that God is, among other things, perfect, changeless, absolutely good and righteous, unspeakably holy, and completely sovereign over his creation. Hence God has strong opinions and feelings about evil, suffering and unrighteousness. If he didn't, we would have grounds for questioning his moral character. God cannot let evil pass. He must deal with it, for while he is loving and merciful, he is also *just.*

Thus God could justly obliterate all sinful and ungodly people in an instant, destroying them forever or punishing them brutally with a single word of command. But this would be inconsistent with his love and mercy. What God has chosen instead is to give all of us a chance to repent. And the basis and condition for that repentance is staggering—God chose to absorb the penalty for sin himself by becoming human and offering up the very incarnation of himself as payment for the penalty of our evil. This, of course, is what the crucifixion of Jesus Christ is all about. God sealed the facts of his victorious love and forgiveness when Christ rose from the dead. This love and forgiveness is available to all who will acknowledge and receive it. "We beseech you on behalf of Christ, be reconciled to God. For our sake he [God] made him [Jesus] *to be sin* who knew no sin, so that in *him* we might become the righteousness of God" (2 Cor 5:20-21).

Yet there are many who will not respond to God's appeal in Christ. The Scriptures plainly state that these will be judged at the Great White Throne in the Final Judgment (Rev 20:11-15). Exactly how God will judge those who have spurned his offer of mercy and what will be their precise fate are not elaborated upon in the Bible. This is probably just as well, for our human feelings on justice and judgment are biased, emotional and finite, and God does not fuel our speculation with a great many details. Suffice it to say that no one will be condemned unless he or she has freely rejected God's offer of mercy and forgiveness in Jesus Christ.

Therefore, divine judgment understood in the light of the redemption offered in Christ does not raise moral problems; it settles them. God's judgment will be totally just. No one can accuse God of living in an ivory tower and not having empathy or understanding for the human condition. He experienced the full range of problems associated with the human predicament for thirty-three years, and he even knew a slow and agonizing death at the hands of his persecutors. When God renders the final judgment, even the condemned will agree with the verdict. His justice is perfect, and all will concur that they have been justly tried and sentenced, for God knows all things, including the hidden thoughts and intentions of each person's heart (Heb 4:12).[8] So the need for justice, in accord with the nature of God, is met in the offering of God on the cross, and judgment is based on each person's response to God's offer of mercy and forgiveness.

Theism Vs. Monism

In contrast to the personal nature of God which biblical theism posits, the concept of God underlying reincarnation is distinctly impersonal. In fact, the title *God* is not really applicable to the religious traditions of the Orient. The word *God* implies a personal being who creates *ex nihilo* (out of nothing) and stands apart from his creation. As H. O. Wiley states in *Christian Theology*, "In the act of creation God brings forth that which had no existence, and which is different in essence from Himself. ... Creation has its origin in the love of God, and is not a mere metaphysical necessity."[9]

In Hinduism, by contrast, the correct word for the "ground of all being" is *Brahman*, which is not technically translatable into the English word *God*. It is probably derived from the Sanskrit *brhat*, which means "big" or "expanded." In Buddhism the concept of the ultimate is even more vacuous, referred to as the *sunya* ("void"). In either case, the Eastern idea of God is simply that of an impersonal reality which emanates forth from itself as an act of "metaphysical necessity," to use Wiley's phrase. This is succinctly stated in an ancient Hindu scripture, the Taittiriya Upanishad: "Before creation came into existence, Brahman existed as the Unmanifest. From the Unmanifest it created [emanated] the manifest. From itself it brought forth itself."[10]

Thus, the ultimate monism of Eastern religions presents us with a distinct problem in considering justice and judgment: an impersonal God, or universal law, cannot show compassion, manifest righteous indignation, or deal with the problem of moral evil in any specific way. Concepts such as love, forgiveness and justice only have meaning within the context of personality; in fact, morality of any kind can only be measured in personal terms. If there were no people to experience injustice, suffering and cruelty, moral categories would be emptied of their meaning. And only with a proper understanding of a personal God is an ultimate reference point for questions of morality found. We cannot appeal to an impersonal God for justice; a personality is required to form opinions and render judgments. This is the cutting edge of biblical theism—the values which give meaning to our lives are affirmed and intensified by the existence of an infinite, personal God who loves us and actively pursues a relationship with us. Love, mercy and forgiveness find no source in the cold and grinding universe ruled by the law of karma. They are thus theoretically impossible in the world view embraced by reincarnation. As British theologian John Wenham writes, "It is when we see the Creator standing over against his creation, distinct from it, yet controlling every particle of it; loving his children with infinite love, yet hating the evil with infinite hatred, that we see theism in all its glory."[11]

In a short essay, Tim Dailey sums up the problem well: "Karma, the law of action and reaction, differs significantly from the Biblical concept of sin in that there is no Transcendent God of the universe (existing outside yourself) to transgress against. It has been written: 'Karma is the Master Law of the Universe but there is no Lawgiver.' "[12]

Does Karma Really Promote Justice?
If karma worked the way reincarnationists say it does, there might be some truth to their claim that it is just and fair. However, if we take a hard look at the doctrine of karma as it is actually applied to reincarnation, some serious built-in flaws become evident. The basic problem is

twofold: (1) since individual personalities are obliterated after death, the "reincarnated soul" is really another person who is laden with someone else's karma; and (2) there is no guarantee that "bad karma" would not increase at a greater rate than "good karma." These problems may be illustrated by using that perennial example of evil, Adolf Hitler. Reincarnationists generally agree that Hitler would be reincarnated many times—perhaps through six million lives, which would correspond to the number of his victims in the concentration camps—and that he would in each life have to suffer agonies similar to those he inflicted.

Here the first problem becomes evident. Hitler died in 1945; let us suppose that he was reborn in 1947 as a crippled baby named Edgar Jones. Edgar, who was born in New York, has no idea that he is really Adolf Hitler reincarnated or that he is suffering for the crimes of the Nazi Führer. It is at this point that justice breaks down totally, for the truth of the matter is that only Adolf Hitler can work off his karma and be punished for his evil deeds. But he is gone, since his personality actually ceased to exist in 1945, and little Edgar Jones now bears the massive burden of Hitler's karmic debt. Hitler thus cheats the hangman while Edgar is victimized. There is a fundamental difference between this "justice" and justice as we know it. Put a man in jail or execute him, and at least he will know what he is being punished for; society will be fairly avenged. With reincarnation, however, society and the individuals suffer meaninglessly.

When Edgar dies, another person is born with Hitler's karma, and so the process is repeated millions of times. (If all the deaths of World War 2 are attributed to Hitler, the total reaches sixty million; if we include the millions of grievously wounded and crippled and the many who were scarred psychologically and emotionally, the total will reach millions more in lost or ruined lives.) Thus Hitler's sin is not paid for by Adolf Hitler, the perpetrator of the crime. Instead the effects of his sins are multiplied through the further suffering of millions in future reincarnations.

The second aspect of karmic justice comes into focus with this multiplication of Hitler's foul deeds. Instead of 60 million innocent victims, we now have many more innocent victims, since the "reincarnations" of Hitler are all doomed to suffer as horribly as the original victims did. This is sheer madness, a living hell spreading like a contagious disease. Again, there is no guarantee that Hitler's karma could be contained or "worked out" in his successive reincarnations, for the bitter pill of this continual suffering would probably have a chain-reaction effect, causing bitterness and ill will to spread, perhaps even producing more Hitlers; in any event his karma could hardly be contained and might spread infectiously throughout the universe in an eternal nightmare of spiritual bubonic plague.

Hence the theory of karma offers neither personal nor cosmic justice. On the personal level, "Edgar" is victimized for the malevolence of Adolf. On the cosmic scale, burgeoning evil thoroughly outweighs the good as bad karma self-generates through repeated incarnations. Here we observe a logical contradiction in the reincarnation theory which would have ultimate harmony evident in the universe: How can karmic balance of good and evil ever be maintained when one man's evil so generates further evil? And, of course, Hitler is only one of many self-centered brutes and violent evildoers.

The problem of reconciling karma and justice is, however, even more problematic. Even by gnostic and reincarnationist definitions, the vast majority of humanity are living in "ignorance" or "illusion" and therefore are not living in harmony with cosmic truth, even if they are not so bad as Hitler. Consequently, most of the people on our beleaguered planet are (and always have been) generating substantially more bad karma than good. If karma and reincarnation are true, we might ask why the world has not been flooded by bad karma and destroyed thousands of years ago. Furthermore, what is "good karma"? In Hinduism and Buddhism it is usually connected with specific spiritual practice, such as yoga and meditation, which dispel ignorance and allow the soul to become enlightened by becoming aware of its inherently divine status. Sometimes it is defined more in the Western sense as just "good works," or abstention from badness, but even here it is slippery and elusive, as the following Hindu example from the *Hitopadesa* shows.

In *The Tale of the Banana Peel,* a Brahmin (a man of Hinduism's highest caste) is ambling along a sidewalk when he comes upon a banana peel lying in the middle of his path. At first he decides to walk around it, not bothering to pick it up. Then he has second thoughts, realizing that the slick peel may cause someone else to slip and fall, perhaps resulting in injury. So the Brahmin says to himself, " 'Every man reaps in the future the fruits of all his acts. If therefore I take this peel from the pathway, I shall have done a deed of merit, and be rewarded by karma in my next life.' So mused the Brahmin and he carefully removed the peel. *For this crafty thought of self,* the proud Brahmin was born in a lower caste in his next life" (emphasis mine).[13]

This little story underscores the rarity with which truly good karma is produced; if only those motivations and acts which are conceived in the utmost selflessness and purity of heart qualify for good karma, it is rare indeed. Or, as G. K. Chesterton has dryly observed, "The one doctrine of Christianity which is empirically verifiable is the fallenness of man." Indeed, as any objective observer of human nature will perceive, the great majority of our motivations are intimately connected with self-gratification. Consequently bad karma, it would seem, always far outweighs good. If karma is synonymous with justice and the vindication of good over evil, it seems to be sorely in need of redefinition.

8
Philosophical and Moral Objections to Reincarnation

THE OVERALL PURPOSE OF reincarnation is to work off all bad karma until the "sound of silence," that is, the primordial state of the universe, returns once more. There are fundamental problems with this thesis. First, it assumes that things are getting better; second, when the end of the karmic phase is reached, it will begin all over again.

Toward the Sound of Silence

The assumption that good karma is increasing is a highly questionable notion, as illustrated in the previous chapter. Since most people live in "ignorance," pursuing self-gratification, bad karma would seemingly be generated at a faster rate than good karma. India bears tragic witness to the problems associated with this thesis; despite all her poverty, starvation, suffering and chaos, India is the land where reincarnation has been taught the longest and most systematically. Since most Indian religion aims at reversing the effects of bad karma, it would seem that the subcontinent should be well along the road of evolutionary progress and be a lighthouse for the world. Yet the exact opposite is true; India's problems are intractable and seemingly without cure.

Even Madame Blavatsky has admitted that karma does seem to be "absurd" and "unfair." She explains that only the Eastern sages have figured it out. But even though she concedes that karma spreads exponentially, she does not pursue the ramifications of her own statement: "Hurt a man by doing him bodily harm; you think that his pain and suffering cannot spread by any means to his neighbors, least of all to other nations. We affirm *that it will, in good time*" (Blavatsky's emphasis).[1]

Head and Cranston also address the problem: "Objectors to reincarnation nevertheless often ask: If all of us have lived thousands of lives, why are we not much further advanced? Such questions usually equate reincarnation with progress, whereas it only provides the opportunity for progress."[2] Thus they admit that reincarnation does not guarantee progress. Just how the present syndrome of rapidly multiplying bad karma will ever be reversed to reach the equilibrium of the sound of silence is never adequately explained by any reincarnationist.

This leads to the second problem. Even if all evil and ignorance were eventually "burned off" and the universe reverted to its original equilibrium, the whole cycle would start all over again in the future. Karma is a *permanent* thing. At best it is only inactive for periods of time. All the gurus, and even Madame Blavatsky, would be reincarnated afresh with the next spasmodic lurch of the wounded cosmos.

This state of affairs gives rise to a rather fundamental question: *Is it desirable to be born again?* If the world is dominated by suffering and ignorance, as seems to be the case, would anyone of sound mind want to experience hundreds or thousands of human lives? The witness of history speaks tragically to this question. Most people down through the years have lived lives of anxiety, boredom, suffering or terror. True, not all people have suffered greatly, but most have lived lives of considerable struggle and hardship, especially by modern Western standards.

Of course, no one wants to believe that despair dominates human existence, and so hope is a persistent theme in human experience and is expressed in whatever context people find themselves.[3] Ian Stevenson, writing in the introduction to Edward Ryall's book *Born Twice,* says, "Edward Ryall's case, like others of its type that I consider genuine, conveys something of which we all stand in need —hope . . . the idea of a second time around suggests both hope and an incentive to better conduct. . . . If John Fletcher has become Edward Ryall in a new body, therein lies hope for the rest of us."[4]

This hope may sound reasonable to some people, but it fades in comparison to the Christian hope of the consummation of life through resurrection, with eternal fulfillment and the destruction of evil and suffering described in the book of Revelation: "Behold, the dwelling of God is with men. He will dwell with them, and they shall be his people, and God himself will be with them; he will wipe away every tear from their eyes, and death shall be no more, neither shall there be mourning nor crying nor pain any more, for the former things have passed away" (21:3-4).

The Obliteration of Personality

Author John Weldon sums up another objection to the idea of reincarnation: "There is only one thing that makes a future life worthwhile—the preservation of the consciousness of personal identity and uniqueness. Yet, in reincarnation, personal identity and uniqueness are forever obliterated."[5] Personality means little in the context of classic Eastern reincarnation. All personalities are ultimately interchangeable and therefore more or less synonymous when viewed over the course of thousands of reincarnations. The universe is one big interconnected unit, and everybody seemingly suffers for everything. Personal responsibility for one's own actions vanishes. Each person bears the allotment of karma that was generated by someone else, and the personality one gets in a particular life therefore seems to be dependent on a throw of the cosmic dice. If reincarnation is true, Adolf Hitler will never have to pay for his crimes, for he has ceased to exist. Instead completely new, unknowing and innocent personalities inherit Hitler's karma. Likewise the righteous also cease to exist, never reaping the benefits of their good lives and self-sacrifice. Others reap the reward.

Ironically, many of the common people of India seem to understand this intuitively. I once asked a Christian pastor in West Bengal whether reincarnation posed any problem for him in his ministry. He replied, "No, because many Indians understand that in reincarnation your personality does not survive. It is destroyed and a new one created. So, in reincarnationist terms, at least, you don't have to worry that your deeds will follow you to the grave—or past it."

How is it possible to derive meaning for life from a stance which teaches obliteration of personality? For everything we are, everything we hope for, is to be found within the context of *personal* existence. To speak of humanity and of human fulfillment is to speak in terms of personality. This is especially true of spiritual salvation. To say that annihilation of personality is a soteriological end cuts across the grain of everything we hope for. Even if self-annihilation were the stated and desired goal, as it is in Buddhism, it is only through personal, cognitive conceptualization that such a hope is formulated. To put it another way, "Without a thinker, the thought is nonexistent." Insisting that annihilation of personality is the highest good is simply an a posteriori argument of conceptual fantasy, put forth by people who are unhappy with life. As Carl Henry says, "A lapse of self-consciousness can only mean the surrender of any personal knowledge whatever."[6]

Thus the truth of the matter is that death for the reincarnationist is not a great deal different from death for an atheist, since individual personality is obliterated. Reincarnation doctrine would suggest that there is no heaven, but only a series of vaguely related life sentences, and that salvation occurs not in an afterlife paradise but with a successful death. MacGregor seems to agree: "Between one life and the next, every single observable characteristic by which we identify people, and even by which we identify ourselves, undergoes a change. How then can we prove that we are really dealing with the same person? . . . For those who fear death as extinction, [reincarnation] gives little context and meaning to the idea of survival."[7]

If reincarnation has little regard for the individuality of persons who are mere bearers of karma from one birth to the next, it has even less regard for the flesh that bears it. A low regard for the physical creation has long been a basic presupposition of pantheist and gnostic philosophies. For example, the Hindu Upanishads state that "this body arises from sexual intercourse. It passes to development in darkness. Then it comes forth through the urinary opening. It is built up with bones; smeared over with flesh; covered with skin, filled with feces, urine, phlegm, marrow, fat, grease and also with many diseases."[8] MacGregor, commenting on this text, says, "What a wretched hybrid must be that reincarnating self! It would seem to be . . . like an ugly bluebottle hopping from one animal excrement to another."[9]

Past-Life Amnesia
In the previous section I have tried to show that the theory of obliteration of personality renders reincarnation unjust. This criticism demonstrates the internal inconsistency of reincarnation, for it purports to be a theory offering thorough justice, whereas in fact great injustice is done to every existing person—each of whom receives the "reward,"

good or bad, of someone else because personality is obliterated at death.

The vacuous nature of the reincarnating self, however, poses a second problem with reincarnation: the inability to remember past lives. This is a practical problem that arises out of the very desire of reincarnationists to make the theory just. If reincarnation were true and we could remember past lives, then we would have to admit the justice of our present lot in life. So past-life recall is more than a fad to reincarnationists; it is an attempt to vindicate the theory's claim to justice. Thus the interest in past-life recall is twofold. First, if we can recall past lives, they must have been real; therefore reincarnation would be true. Second, if we can recall past lives, then we know we are fairly treated in life; therefore reincarnation would be just.

Not all reincarnationists cite memory of past lives as a proof of reincarnation, but since the inability to remember past lives is manifestly evident for the vast majority of the population, some reincarnationists are understandably defensive about it. Occult apologist Arthur Robson offers a standard reply: "The common objection to the theory of reincarnation is 'Why don't we remember our past lives?' It's true that ordinarily we cannot recall any part of our past lives, but in everything we do our past is plainly seen. Obvious examples are the natural inclinations of each of us . . . outstanding among them being great musicians, artists, mathematicians, etc."[10]

Here the writer avoids the question he has just asked, using words like *plainly* and *obvious,* expecting the reader to believe that the very existence of talented people proves reincarnation. Leoline Wright gives another reincarnationist answer: "The fact is that we *do* remember them." Her explanation is equally spurious, as she states that good character in a person "proves" that that individual has learned his or her lesson from past lives. "In this way we can say that character is memory."[11]

By any accounting, however, not many of us (if any at all) remember past lives. Even Wright says that "John Smith and Mary Brown are not deathless beings. They are mere personalities, and as such do not reincarnate."[12] If personality is obliterated at death, how can it be remembered and experienced in a future life? Those reincarnationists who firmly hold to the obliteration of personality do not look for recall experiences, believing the earlier incarnation to be gone—and all access to it, even by memory, to be gone as well. Madame Blavatsky finally admits as much: "It may be said that there is not a mental or physical suffering in the life of a mortal which is not the direct fruit and consequence of some sin in a preceding existence; *on the other hand, he does not preserve the slightest recollection of it in his actual life*" (emphasis mine).[13]

What are we to make of this? Each individual personality is supposedly responsible for his or her actions, but neither pays the penalty nor gets the reward, since the personality is extinguished. A totally different person is reborn, burdened with someone else's karma. The questions remain. Does this make sense? Is it just and fair? More important still, is reincarnation really true, or just the product of thousands of years of human speculation? Walter Martin comments on the problem:

It's very interesting that the reincarnationist tells us we go through cyclic rebirth and we suffer in various lives to atone for our sins. But it's very puzzling that nobody remembers his past life in enough detail to profit from it! So we don't know what we're being punished for. And if we don't know what we're being punished for, we're quite likely to repeat the offense. If reincarnation is really karma, or the law of justice ("as you sow, so shall you reap"), why not protect the person? Why not give him a full vision of what he had been before, with all his flaws, so that the necessary corrections could be made?[14]

Paternoster touches the heart of the matter when he says, "With rare exceptions, we seem to have no memory of previous existences. This is not only an argument against the truth of reincarnation, *it is also an argument against its utility,* if true" (emphasis mine).[15]

Moral Objections to Reincarnation

While philosophic matters and questions of internal logic raise serious doubts about the reality of reincarnation, it is just as important to look at the moral implications of reincarnation teachings.

One such consequence of reincarnation teachings is moral procrastination. Since one always gets "another chance"—whatever that may mean within the impersonal framework of reincarnation—moral imperatives are less urgent, reminding us of Augustine's preconversion prayer, "Give me chastity, but not yet." While a little procrastination may not seem too harmful, this attitude is intrinsically tied to a muted view of the reality of evil and suffering. Nothing is urgent since the cosmic drama of life must unfold according to predetermined karmic fate. People are perceived as merely "working out their karma," and many reincarnationists feel it is unwise to disturb the process. As a result, people who are suffering are left to their fate until their karma is exhausted. However one may mask this callous attitude by appealing to higher consciousness or karmic law, it ultimately is manifested as *a low regard for individual life*—which often sears both conscience and compassion.

This low regard for human life is well illustrated in the Bhagavad-Gita. Arjuna, a warrior by caste, finds himself in a genuine predicament. He must engage his kinsmen in war. Although he loves them, he realizes that it is his divine duty to fight because of his caste responsibility. As he anguishes on the battlefield, torn between duty and compassion, the god Krishna appears to him and says,

Abandon this despicable weakness of thy heart and stand up.... Thou grievest for those who may not be lamented.... I myself was not, not thou, nor all the princes of the earth; nor shall we ever hereafter cease to be. As the Lord of this mortal frame experienceth therein infancy, youth and old age, so in future incarnations will it meet the same. One who is confirmed in this belief is not disturbed by anything that may come to pass.[16]

In other words, Krishna has just told Arjuna that he may feel free to kill his kinsmen in battle, for he is not really killing them; he is only destroying the "mortal frame," which is of no great importance since the soul will incarnate again.

This advice is based on the pivotal Hindu concept of *dharma,* which may be roughly translated as "the inevitability of what must be," or "doing what is set before you." "It is the dharma of fire to burn," as the Indian saying goes. The heart of the matter is that dharma is the unfolding of the divine plan, and therefore there is ultimately neither good nor evil. These categories are obliterated when one attains enlightenment and sees the perfection of all that exists. In Hindu thought, evil is an illusion, an attachment to the phenomenal world which is continually evolving and passing away. Good is therefore synonymous with enlightenment—specifically, that which serves to detach the soul from the worldly illusion of separate and individual existence. The truly enlightened soul realizes that he or she is only a mode of God's existence. Good and evil are not seen as absolute moral categories as they are in Christianity; they are merely different and complementary facets of the divine nature.

This aspect of monism is illustrated very well in the Hindu scripture, the Svetasvatara Upanishad, where we see the concept of enlightenment inextricably bound with reincarnation: "This vast universe is a wheel. Upon it are all creatures that are subject to birth, death and rebirth.

Round and round it turns, and never stops. It is the wheel of Brahman. As long as the individual self thinks it is separate from Brahman, it revolves upon the wheel in bondage to the laws of birth, death and rebirth."[17]

Therefore, just as it is the dharma of fire to burn, each individual's dharma, or fate, is sealed by his karmic inheritance as it evolves its way slowly back to the Godhead. It is all part of the divine play, or *lila,* which goes as it must.

Consequently, dharma strongly implies a predeterminism which binds each soul to its respective load of karma. This is illustrated in the Bhagavad-Gita when Yudhishthira, older brother of the hero Arjuna, tries to get a straight answer about the problem of predetermined dharma from Krishna, the incarnation of Absolute Deity. Instead he gets only an evasive half-answer because his time for enlightenment has not yet arrived. R. C. Zaehner comments on the passage:

> When the battle is over and won, he [Arjuna] asks Krishna whether he would be good enough to repeat them [the words of esoteric saving knowledge] since their purport has gone clear out of his head! Why, one wonders, did the Incarnate God elect to waste his words on Arjuna rather than on Yudhishthira who was athirst to hear them? . . . Yudhishthira's karma has not yet worked itself out: he must wait for it to "ripen" and only then will he attain to moksha [liberation]. To tell him the great secret prematurely would be to violate dharma itself, for the law of karma is inseparable from the eternal dharma and not even God can break it.[18]

In other words, Arjuna's karma, buried in previous lives, had somehow qualified him for Krishna's saving words; Yudhishthira, despite his desperate desire for truth, was spiritually hamstrung by unremembered karma from past lives, karma so binding and unremitting that not even Krishna, as God incarnate, could release him.

The Neo-Platonic philosopher Plotinus (A.D. 205-270)

expresses similar sentiments as those found in the Gita:

It [death] comes to no more than the murder of one of the personages in a play; the actor alters his make-up and enters in a new role. The actor, of course, was not really killed; but if dying is but changing a body as the actor changes a costume, or even an exit from the body like the exit of an actor from the boards when he has no more to say or do, what is there so very dreadful in the transformation of living beings one into another? Murders, death in all its guises, the reduction and sacking of cities, all must be just a spectacle as the changing scenes in a play; all is but the varied incident of a plot, costume on and off, acted grief and lament. . . . All this is the doing of man, knowing and never perceiving that in his weeping and in his graver doings alike, he is but at play.[19]

As might be expected, this view has some rather sinister outworkings. It negates not only absolute moral values, but even *relative* moral values. For instance, hypnotherapist Edith Fiore says, "The therapist should have a metaphysical background too. If she finds a patient murdered his sister in a past life, *she has to help him understand that these incidents are just lessons. Just like the child in school who fails, the failure doesn't mean he's good or bad, just that he failed the lesson*" (emphasis mine).[20]

A more blatant example is that uttered by one John-Roger, a Los Angeles "spiritual leader" who is head of the syncretist "Movement of Spiritual Inner Awareness" (MSIA):

Let's look at the Vietnamese people for the last 3,000 years of their existence. As a collective group, they may have gotten exactly what they created for themselves, and they may have balanced all of their karma. Now, is it bad for them to be karmically free of all that? Is that wrong? Perhaps that particular freedom didn't come about in a really popular way, in terms of what we all might have wanted it to be, but it came about in a way that was entirely perfect. There was no overkill; there was no underkill. The Americans that went over there and were caught up in it were part of the Vietnamese process thousands of years ago, and even though they were born in America this life, they were pulled back there to complete their karma, also. And those who went through the war unharmed were not part of the process and came home safely. So how can that action be judged as "wrong"?[21]

If we are to accept John-Roger's judgment, the war in Viet Nam was a cosmic necessity as it balanced a lot of karma. How much more fulfilling, then, was the holocaust of World War 2, in which millions were tortured and roasted, their skins made into lampshades! If ever there were a notion more morally repugnant than this, it would be hard to find. The Scriptures testify:

Woe to those who call evil good
  and good evil,
who put darkness for light
  and light for darkness,
who put bitter for sweet
  and sweet for bitter! (Is 5:20)

If reincarnation is true, there is little reason for comforting one another when misfortune overtakes us. Imagine saying to a young couple with a deformed infant: "It's no problem. Look at it in the cosmic perspective. He must have been a horrible person in the past life, perhaps one of Stalin's executioners, a murderer, or even Attila the Hun." The response is not hard to imagine; and such ghoulish and tasteless speculation could be applied to every unfortunate situation of life. Little wonder that in the East misfortune is met with resignation.

9
Theological Objections

ONE OF THE FIRST CHRISTIANS to engage in a serious study of comparative religions was Irenaeus, Bishop of Lyons. During the latter part of the second century, the Gnostics and other mystery religions had become a serious problem for the churches in southern Gaul, and Irenaeus took the offensive by writing several lengthy treatises in defense of the faith. The bishop was well aware of the exotic appeal of "hidden wisdom" which was part of the Gnostic message. In the preface to his monumental work *Against Heresies,* he wrote: "Error, indeed, is never set forth in its naked deformity, lest, being thus exposed, it should at once be detected. But it is craftily decked out in attractive dress, so as, by its outward form, to make it appear to the inexperienced more true than the truth itself."[1]

One of the ablest of the church fathers, Irenaeus understood that the best way to refute the Gnostic system was to critique it from within rather than simply to shout invectives at it. Through his intensive study he became more conversant in Gnosticism than even some of the Gnostics themselves. In like fashion we need to understand thoroughly the philosophy of reincarnation before we can come to intelligent conclusions about it. Having examined the outward teachings of reincarnation, we should direct our attention now to the underlying metaphysical bedrock—the theology of reincarnation.

It may be said with some certainty that no religion or religious philosophy is any better than its conception of God. Reincarnation is based upon the Eastern view of God and the universe, which as I have explained, is often called gnostic or occult mysticism, or monism. In a spiritual framework, monism always refers to the idea that "All is One," the idea that God is not separate from the creation. *Occult,* in its most basic etymological sense, is derived from the Latin meaning "hidden," a concept similar to the *gnosis* of Gnosticism; both terms refer to the secret doctrines and practices of mysticism whereby a person may come to enlightenment or realization that he or she is of the same essence as "God," or the "Absolute," the ethereal substratum from which all creation emanates.

There are two fundamental problems with the doctrine of theological monism. First, it is not really theology. We have always known that the universe exists; to simply change its name from "universe" to "God" is a meaningless tautology and does not answer the real questions of the origin and purpose of the world or the nature of God. Second, the "God" of monism is fatally flawed. Since he (or "it," which is more accurate) is of one essence with creation and consciousness, God is thus the origin of the imperfection and evil in our world; the foulest deeds and thoughts of humanity literally become attributes of God.

A chain is only as strong as its weakest link. The God of monism is by definition the actual perpetrator of imperfection, evil and suffering, as all things proceed out of its very being as an emanation at the beginning of creation. This fact is usually not confronted by monists, but even when it is, it is rarely pursued. Theosophist Clarence Pedersen, in his article "The Source of Becauses," does admit that "Karma must have come into operation with the first instant of manifestation, the first instant of creation."[2] Unfortunately, Pedersen never follows his statement through to its logical conclusion, namely, *that the creation and the Fall are synonymous and simultaneous;* while he does tacitly admit that his Deity is imperfect and limited in power, it apparently makes little difference: "God, we may say, observing what he has wrought, immediately repents his rashness. *Unable to recall* that portion of his consciousness which he has willed forth, he now does the next best thing and proceeds to negate the effects of First Cause" (emphasis mine).[3]

Pedersen's description of creation only underscores the fundamental problem in monism. The Deity is under compulsion to manifest itself in the created order, much like a dam that is about to burst. It cannot be constrained and has limited power to control the creation process once it starts; thus it is neither omnipotent nor omniscient, and the goodness and holiness of such a God is certainly subject to question. Once the power, holiness and goodness of God are done away with, creation becomes an unqualified hell.

The inability of monists to perceive this crucial flaw stems from the ultimate amorality of their philosophy. Good and evil as mutually exclusive moral categories are said to be only an "illusion" which blinds humanity from seeing the unity of all things. Thus the ultimate achievement is to rise to a "higher state of consciousness" where one is unencumbered by such crude stumbling stones as "good" and "evil."

While all this has an appearance of "wisdom" and is often propagated as such, it is in fact nothing more than "error craftily decked out in attractive dress," as Irenaeus observed eighteen hundred years ago. Perhaps it would be closer to the mark to say that such a notion is one of the most monumental intellectual and moral defaults in the history of human thought. It should be noted that the inability to distinguish between right and wrong is a legal definition of *insanity* according to most systems of jurisprudence. When a murderer is declared not guilty by reason of insanity, it means that he did not know it was wrong to kill his victim.

This idea of an uncontrolled Deity mired in its own creation undergirds the system of reincarnation and karma. All lives partake of the balancing act in which people, as part of the One, redeem the universe. But in the final analysis it never is redeemed; as the Buddhist Slokas say, "The thread of radiance which is imperishable and dissolves only in Nirvana, re-emerges from it on the day when the Great Law calls all things back into action." Thus the law of karma only postpones the solution to the problem of evil and suffering eternally, without ever confronting or solving the root of the dilemma.

Reincarnation and Theodicy

On the surface, the doctrine of reincarnation is an honest human attempt to answer the problem of *theodicy*, God's relationship to evil. For this reason many people find it appealing. W. R. Alger, a distinguished Unitarian clergyman of the nineteenth century, enthusiastically shared this view: "The theory of transmigration of souls is marvellously adapted to explain the seeming chaos of moral inequity, injustice and manifold evil presented in the world of human life. Once admit the theory to be true, and all the difficulties in regard to moral justice vanish."[4]

In the first half of his statement Alger makes a valid point: reincarnation does provide a specific explanation for situations of injustice, inequality and suffering. The victimized person has committed offenses in previous lives and must therefore pay the consequences. It is a theory which very much appeals to the deep questions of people who cry out and ask "Why?" or "Why me?"

But herein lies the danger. It is an attempt to reduce the deepest and most painful human questions and problems to an easily manageable formula. While it does provide a convenient solution to the problem of injustice and suffering, it only pushes the real problem of theodicy and the origin of evil further out of reach and perpetuates it through endless cycles of karmic action and reaction.

The second half of Alger's statement, his remark that "all difficulties in regard to moral justice vanish," is both naive and incorrect. For even if we are able to account for the unjust suffering of individuals, the root problem of the origin of evil remains. Nor does the philosophic system on which reincarnation is based ever provide any *final solution* to the problem of evil and suffering; for each new regeneration of the universe gives rise to the same old status quo. In this respect reincarnation is a totally inadequate response to the problem of evil.

The Christian faith approaches the problem of evil and suffering quite differently. Instead of indicating a specific reason for each person's individual plight, biblical revelation appeals to the sovereignty and mercy of God. This is well illustrated in the story of the man born blind (Jn 9:1-3). When specifically asked about this very problem ("Who sinned, this man or his parents, that he was born blind?"), Jesus did not engage in past-life speculations: "It was not that this man sinned, or his parents, but that the works of God might be made manifest in him." Jesus then restored his sight. The man's individual situation is viewed as a symptom of the total human condition, which Jesus came to redeem. Why the blind man had suffered more than others we are not told.

Paul also addressed this problem in the book of Romans: "What shall we say then? Is there injustice on God's part? By no means! . . . But who are you, a man, to answer back to God? Will what is molded say to its molder, 'Why have you made me thus?' Has the potter no right over the clay, to make out of the same lump one vessel for beauty and another for menial use?" (9:14, 20-21). Paul responds to the problem by appealing to the sovereignty of God as expressed in Christian theism: God is the all-powerful and all-wise Creator, a personal God who actively wills things, as opposed to the impersonal God of reincarnationists that is in bondage to its own nature in perpetuity. In Romans 11:33-34, the apostle rests his case:

O the depth of the riches and wisdom and knowledge of God! How unsearchable are his judgments and how inscrutable his ways!

"For who has known the mind of the Lord, or who has been his counselor?"

Who then are we to presume to understand the infinite wisdom and complexity of the divine purposes? God's plan will unfold perfectly and in its time; it is our duty to love and obey him. It is our desire to place ourselves at the center of the universe and be as God that has been our undoing.

At this point some may still ask how Christianity is any different when it comes to the problem of God and evil. Is not the God of the Bible also responsible for evil? Although God is of course "responsible" for everything that transpires in his universe, it is more precise to say that he *responds* to evil. But evil is not part of his character. While the Scriptures do not give us a precise, systematic statement on the origin of evil (theodicy is primarily addressed in terms of its *solution,* the cross of Christ), they do provide a number of pieces to put together this greatest of puzzles. This subject, needless to say, deserves several volumes; I can at most supply a skeletal outline.

Primarily, it is generally held that God created sentient beings so they could share in his love and goodness through a personal relationship with him. Yet love involves choice and free will; if we were not free to love God, but only programmed like robots, love would not be genuine. And free will involves risk; it may be abused. Apparently it was abused. Satan, for reasons that are little understood, rebelled against God in what was probably a sin of pride and self-will. He led a rebellion and was exiled to earth with his fallen angels. When the human race was created, they were seduced by Satan and hence came the Fall.

The important concept to grasp here is that evil did not originate with God; he is not the author of evil, although he has allowed it to continue for a season for reasons finally known only to him. His moral perfection is thereby preserved. Although God could obliterate all his fallen creatures with one sharp command, he has instead chosen to prove his love by becoming incarnate as one of us, experientially sharing our suffering and personally paying the price by redeeming the stricken race. This is the true love and character of God made known. Thus the Lord told the apostle Paul, "My grace is sufficient for you, for my power is made perfect in weakness" (2 Cor 12:9).

In this light it seems clear that the monistic doctrine of dissolution of personality is in actuality an attack upon the personal nature of God himself. While God is infinite, unsearchable and ineffable, as Paul declares in Romans 11, he is also the same God who revealed himself to Moses by the Hebrew name of *Yahweh* ("I AM WHAT I AM"). The oft-quoted verse in Genesis 1:26, that God made humanity in his own image, is generally held to refer to *personality;* we who are finite-personal beings can know God because he is infinite-personal. When personality is destroyed and obliterated, no amount of clever sophistry can disguise the fact that "God" is reduced to an existential blur or a sinking feeling in the pit of one's stomach. God is then lowered to an object of philosophical musing; "he" becomes a scientifically defined cosmic law which can be manipulated by spiritual techniques instead of worshiped.

Law and Grace

Theologian Francis Schaeffer once said that if each person were to go through life with a tape recorder hung around his or her neck, everyone would stand condemned at the Final Judgment when the reels were played back; for each of us would pass sentence on ourselves for being guilty of doing the very things we daily decried. Such is the human condition. We have all broken God's laws, ignored him in self-pursuit, and deserve the punishment (Rom 3:23 and 6:23). Likewise, according to reincarnationists, we have all become enmeshed in the law of karma. As Blavatsky says,

> Our philosophy has a doctrine of punishment as stern as that of the most rigid Calvinist, only far more consistent, and philosophical, with absolute justice. No deed, not even a single thought, will go unpunished; the latter more severely even than the former, as a thought has far more potential in creating evil results even than a deed.[5]

The law of karma is a hard taskmaster, and every soul must bear its own burden. Blavatsky confirms this when she says, "[Reincarnation] is the destiny of every Ego, which thus becomes its own Savior in each world and incarnation."[6] In *Travel Diary of a Philosopher*, Count Hermann Keyserling concurs:

> Every action entails, according to the law of karma, its natural and inevitable consequence; every one must bear those for himself, no merciful Providence can remove them.... The man who does not believe in himself is considered to be an atheist in the real sense of the word. The highest ideal would be if a man could think of himself continuously, not as the most sinful of sinners ... but as perfect; such a man would no doubt attain perfection even in this life.[7]

How anyone would attain perfection by thinking only of himself is an incomprehensible anomaly, but at any rate it becomes obvious that there are no free lunches in reincarnation.

The concepts of mercy and forgiveness are foreign to the cosmic gristmill of karmic thought, although the teaching of Buddhism concerning *bodhisattvas* bears a surface resemblance. These bodhisattvas are reincarnated masters who are said to possess the ability to burn off inordinate amounts of the karma of their followers if their disciples submit totally to their teaching and techniques. This state of affairs is not, however, to be confused with forgiveness; it is more like an acceleration process. Furthermore, the bodhisattvas are limited in their influence by time and space and must reincarnate periodically. Since this concept postdates Hebrew thought, it may be a modification of the forgiveness taught in the Old Testament. Similarly, Hinduism has had since medieval times its *avatars,* who are said to be "mini-incarnations" that arrive from time to time in the form of holy men.

In stark contrast, Christian love knows nothing of calculations or boundaries. The fallen human condition is not a closed system that perpetuates itself into eternity with no exit. Geddes MacGregor observes:

Asiatic religions, which have rightly been called "religions of eternal cosmic law" imply a state of affairs that orthodox Christians have always believed to be that which Jesus Christ came to end. There is truth in the slogan of some modern theologians that Christianity is not a religion, but the end of religions. That is, indeed, precisely what the primitive church saw behind the Death and Resurrection of Christ.... So there is a dimension in the Christian faith that no karmic principle or reincarnationist doctrine could fully contain, since Jesus Christ is held to be victorious over the very state of affairs they represent.[8]

Reincarnationists say we are all working our way back to God; Christianity says that we are running away from God but that he has pursued us in Jesus Christ. "But God shows his love for us in that while we were yet sinners

Christ died for us" (Rom 5:8). It is he who redeems us.

Martin Luther called this human predicament "the bondage of the will." Calvin put it in stronger terms, speaking of humanity's "total depravity." Both men meant that the human race is hopelessly enslaved to self-will, "making man the measure of all things" and caring little, if anything, for the will of God unless it can be manipulated for self-gratification. In responding to this condition, God undertakes responsibility for his rebellious creatures, taking the initiative by actually absorbing the sin of humanity and its consequences: "For our sake he [God] made him to be sin who knew no sin [Christ], so that in him we might become the righteousness of God" (2 Cor 5:21).

Thus we have the "big switch" of Christian theology. God takes our sin, condemns it on the cross and gives us his righteousness in return as grace, a free and undeserved gift. Because it is accomplished and given by God, it is perfect and complete; nothing can be added to it, and human righteousness and good works cannot improve God's forgiveness.

In fact, one of the greatest misconceptions that can be held about the nature of God is that he does not forgive sin—a thesis that the proponents of reincarnation frequently assert. They do not feel it possible for God to be merciful or for human beings to be personally transformed by the free gift of his grace and mercy. Sadly, this is a common misconception among people of all religions. It has been said that human religion is no more than people trying to reach up and appease God through feeble works of self-righteousness and austerities; in contrast, God's religion is initiated by God himself, as he reaches down in self-revelation and forgiveness. For this reason Paul is adamant when he says, "For by grace you have been saved through faith; and this is not your own doing, it is the gift of God—not because of works, lest any man should boast" (Eph 2:8-9).

Even in the Old Testament, centuries before Christ, God held out his hand to all:
Come now, let us reason together,
    says the LORD:
though your sins are like scarlet,
    they shall be as white as snow;
though they are red like crimson,
    they shall become like wool. (Is 1:18)
Let the wicked forsake his way,
    and the unrighteous man his thoughts;
let him return to the LORD, that he may have
      mercy on him,
    and to our God, for he will abundantly pardon.
    (Is 55:7)

Such is the true love of God. Can it even be compared to the merciless and exacting retribution of karma and reincarnation? The gulf is infinitely wide between the two: God has effected a permanent healing, soon to be complete, while reincarnation is an eternally incurable malignancy. Essentially, bad karma is nothing more than unforgiven sin, and, as such it stands in marked contrast to the reality of forgiveness, which is summed up in superlative terms by the words of the wounded horseman: "Betwixt the stirrup and the ground, mercy I asked, mercy I found."

Satan's Last Stand

Scripture tells us that death is the last enemy to be conquered. It was also the first result of the Fall: "For in the day that you eat of [the tree] you shall die" (Gen 2:17). The curse of death is at the very center of the human condition; Jesus validated his claim to be the Messiah by being raised from the dead. Paul tells the Corinthians that if Christ has not been raised, their faith is futile and they are still in their sins. If for this life only they have hoped in Christ, they "are of all men most to be pitied" (1 Cor 15:19). Over and over again, death is held out as the counterpoint to God's offer of life in the Bible.

Because there is so much at stake with death, it is precisely at this point that Satan can be expected to make his final stand. If he could be successful in denying the *reality* of the curse of death, he could anesthetize people to the need for the gospel of the New Testament. Therefore, an all-out assault is likely; the serpent's retort to Eve in the garden has echoed down through the centuries: *"You will not die.* For God knows that when you eat of it your eyes will be opened, and you will be like God" (Gen 3:4-5). His perennial denial of sin and death is perhaps an attempt to justify his rebellion and establish an autonomous set of rules for his own kingdom.

The most recent assault on the reality and the curse of death has secured a firm beachhead through the thanatology movement, popularized by Elisabeth Kübler-Ross with her life-after-death research (she claims to be aided by several helpful spirit beings named Salem, Anka, and Willie), and Raymond Moody with his best seller *Life after Life*. The current boom in popular reincarnation beliefs and past-life recall may catch many a hungry fish with the same old battered lure. Helen Wambach reports that ninety per cent of her subjects experienced "previous deaths" with little or no negative feelings, and often with joy. During a lecture in Palo Alto, California, she summed up the prevailing Zeitgeist with obvious relish: "The Age of Aquarius means that we're learning that we never die. You will experience many lives, many time periods."[9]

Spiritual Deception and Spiritual Warfare
Finally, it must be realized that spiritual deception is the means to an end, and that end is spiritual bondage. Reincarnation is a philosophic/religious system which is the direct antithesis of biblical revelation. Because the concept of rebirth is such a linchpin in gnostic-occult and Eastern philosophy, it has been highly developed, covered over

with layers of sophistry, and reinforced by centuries of elaborate philosophy in order to render it palatable to its followers. However, underneath the sugar coating is the bitter pill of error; recall phenomena are only part of the whole system of spiritual bondage and deception into which entire races and cultures have fallen.

This bondage is exemplified by the after-death rites performed by certain Tibetan Buddhists, who are firm believers in reincarnation. When a person dies, the body is carried to a large flat rock on a hillside by specially trained people known as "dumden men." These men undress the corpse and, laying it out on the rock, methodically butcher the body with machetes. The limbs are first hacked off and stripped of all flesh; the body is decapitated, the flesh is scraped from the skull and the brains are removed. Then the torso is ripped open and disemboweled, and all the human flesh is chopped into bite-sized pieces for the gathering vultures. The remaining bones are ground to a pasty pulp with mortar and pestle and mixed with ghee (clarified yak butter) and barley meal. This mixture is then whipped into a stiff paste and set next to the flesh. The vultures descend and eat. If the ghoulish remains are entirely eaten by the birds, it is a good omen for the reincarnating soul; if uneaten or partially devoured, it bodes evil for the next birth.

Such is the reality of spiritual bondage. The Old Testament strictly forbade similar rituals of pagan cults practiced by Israel's neighbors, rituals such as the burning of one's children as sacrifices. In the New Testament, the apostle Paul, writing to the church in Corinth, asserted that pagan idolatry was more than just folk nonsense. Speaking of the local temple sacrifices, Paul recognized that they were forms of systematic bondage, in which demons were masquerading as beneficent gods:

What do I imply then? That food offered to idols is anything, or that an idol is anything? No, I imply that what pagans sacrifice they offer to demons and not to God. I do not want you to be partners with demons. (1 Cor 10:19-21)

Comparing Religions

In comparing religious world views such as gnostic reincarnation and Christianity, it is helpful to have a frame of reference, a theological grid on which to evaluate belief systems. This enables us more clearly to perceive differences and similarities on critical points. One such grid compares various religions in five main areas of doctrinal concern: (1) doctrine of God, (2) nature of the world, (3) human nature, (4) method of salvation and (5) theodicy.

Comparing the positions of Christianity to the gnostic/reincarnationist views in this way, it becomes obvious that the two are in fundamental disagreement on all these pivotal issues. A brief cross-referencing of the two views will bring the picture into sharper focus.

Doctrine of God. As demonstrated throughout this study, the theology of reincarnation is based on an impersonal principle which undergirds the universe and emanates forth from itself in endless cycles of expansion and contraction. In contrast, the Bible tells us that God is holy and infinite in all respects, yet personal; he is a God who stands apart from creation and loves his creatures with a self-sacrificing love.

Nature of the world. Reincarnation views the world as a state which is less than real, an illusory projection of consciousness which is inherently negative, a lamentable byproduct of the creative forces of the universe. Christianity sees the world as real, though temporal and fallen. It is part of God's deliberate creation, and as such it has a definite purpose and is basically good. The finished creation is portrayed in Genesis (before the Fall) as both real and good.

Human nature. Reincarnation regards people as transient shells that are filled with an immortal soul for a season and then extinguished forever as the soul passes on and assumes a new body and personality. This soul or spiritual essence is conceived of as being a part of God. Christianity views people as made in the image of God (see Genesis 1:26), and so human beings have both personality and moral responsibility. Nonetheless, we are not Deity in essence, and humanity is not a mode of the Divine; an infinite gulf separates creature from the Creator.

Method of salvation. Reincarnationists insist on self-salvation; the soul must save itself by working off karma in multitudinous reincarnations, finally achieving liberation by getting off the wheel of rebirth. Christianity insists that eternal salvation is a gift from God in which the personality is retained, and salvation is conferred on the recipient regardless of merit. It is only necessary to receive the gift of eternal life through faith and then to apply it through righteous living. Jesus' merit becomes our merit.

Theodicy. Reincarnation's endless cycles never solve the problem of evil; evil is eternal. The idea of evil continuing forever is unthinkable in Christianity. Evil was conquered by the death and resurrection of Christ and will be put away forever when he returns to judge the world. This is reflected in Jesus' frequent restatement of the theme "this age [the present order of things] and the age to come [the eradication of evil in the kingdom of God]."

All things considered, a fundamental difference between historic Christianity and the religions of the East lies in their respective focal points. The former puts God at the center; he is the object of worship. The latter reduces theology to anthropology, making humanity the measure of all things. British writer Harry Blamires underscores the danger of this anthropocentric view when he says, "In the Christian moral system the key sin is pride—that perversion of the will by which the self is asserted as the center of the universe. That is the mark of the utterly lost soul."[10]

10
Theological Hybrids

ONE OF THE MOST PERSISTENT challenges to orthodox Christianity is *syncretism,* the idea that all religions say the same thing "in a different language" and that all paths are equally valid in knowing God. The early church fought a long, hard battle against syncretism when Gnosticism, Greek philosophy and the mystery religions tried to assimilate the faith. Ultimately the church was victorious, but not without a number of casualties. Now, eighteen centuries later, we face a similar situation.

Many Christians stand bewildered and confused by the subtle and intricate maze of oriental and humanistic philosophies that are gaining credence in the West. Eastern mysticism and pop occultism mixed with humanistic psychology have already seduced large numbers of nominal Christians onto the broad road to the nether regions. Even many church leaders and theologians have warmly embraced a modified gnostic or pantheistic world view and, with it, reincarnation.[1] Because of these developments, the question needs to be asked again for the sake of summary: Can the doctrine of reincarnation be christened? Does it offer anything that would enrich Christianity? MacGregor observes:

Is it not like baptizing a company's balance sheet or profit and loss account? Everything we are told of Christ, everything that leads the Christian to accept Christ as his or her Savior, tells of a generosity so immense, of a love so selfless, that it has no conceivable place for any such mathematical reckoning [i.e., karma and rebirth]. Typical of the Christian's conversion experience is the awareness that if God were looking for merit, he would certainly look elsewhere.[2]

Rather than try to accommodate various theories of rebirth within Christianity, Paternoster suggests that "perhaps we should be better employed trying to persuade the Orient that it is not a self-evident fact, but a nightmare from which they can awake. Even if we do want to believe it, is there any convincing reason why we should suppose it to be true?"[3]

The biggest barrier to reincarnation for the Christian is not so much the simple concept of being born again and again. It is *conceivable* that rebirth could coexist with biblical doctrines if it were highly sanitized and applied only to unbelievers. What makes reincarnation impossible for Christians is that it cannot be separated from its metaphysical undergirding, the superstructure of gnostic mysticism and monism. Helmut Thielicke saw gnostic mysticism as "a secular theory of immortality," referring to it cryptically as "the ultimate refinement of blasphemy, for it sets God in analogy to man."

Rarely is this blasphemy and overt hostility evidenced more than in some of the writings of Madame Blavatsky. In *Isis Unveiled* she vents her deepest antagonism, calling Jesus "the holy thief of Calvary" and inveighing against Christianity, as she often does:

How strangely illogical is this doctrine of the Atonement.

We propose to discuss it . . . and show that it has proved one of the most pernicious and demoralizing of doctrines . . . the cause of three-fourths of the crimes of so-called Christians. . . . But if we step outside of the little circle of creed and consider the universe as a whole, balanced by the exquisite adjustment of parts, how all sound logic, how the faintest glimmering of sense revolts against this Vicarious Atonement![4]

Blavatsky's polemics are quoted to underscore the overwhelming differences between Christianity and the gnostic world view that nurtures reincarnation. Blavatsky loathed the idea of divine forgiveness, and her opinions are shared by many reincarnationists who are less outspoken. Figure 1 shows how diametrically opposed to one another these two world views are at virtually every major point of doctrine.

It should be rather obvious now that reincarnation is incompatible with the biblical view of God and humanity. As Friedrich Gogarten has aptly said, "Mysticism and historical revelation mutually exclude one another so forcibly that a mixture of them destroys both."[5] Reincarnation obviously cannot be grafted onto Christianity, but neither can it be ignored, for reincarnation presents the only real systematic alternative to the biblical teaching of resurrection. After thousands of years of development and refinement, reincarnation is a highly philosophic and subtle doctrine which seems both reasonable and exotic to the novice spiritual seeker. It is here to stay and is gathering force and credibility in the eyes of many, its appeal strengthened by the influx of Eastern thought and the revival of the ancient Platonic doctrine of immortality of the soul through occultism and psychic research, all of which hold that the eternal life of the soul is a natural component of human nature.

But the truth about immortality is radically different. It is a *gift of God* imparted to the redeemed, by which all who trust in Jesus are *raised* from their natural state of physical and spiritual death. Eternal life is not just the next step of

Gnostic-Pantheistic World View

1. "God" is totally synonymous with creation (monism or pantheism): "All is One," "Thou art that."

2. God is a principle, a universal law, vibration or energy. Universal Consciousness. "It," not "Him." Holy Spirit is an impersonal force.

3. Humanity is good—a part or mode of God. The totality of existence is really good as it is, although we do not perceive this. Moral evil is only an illusion or imperfection, negative vibration or energy. "Evil" is simply a result of the law of cause and effect. "Good and bad" are part of karmic balance. An enlightened person transcends moral distinctions.

4. Christ's death, resurrection and atonement for sin are unnecessary and irrelevant. No forgiveness.

5. View of history and humanity is cyclical. Problem of evil and suffering is never resolved. No redemption, only an eternal balancing of karma.

6. The physical world is illusory, a projection of consciousness: *Maya*, "the veil of ignorance."

7. Works win righteousness. You save yourself by working off your karma, and getting off the wheel of reincarnation.

8. God inherits the imperfection of the world. He/"It" is equal to the lowest form of creation by definition. Or, alternatively, the world mirrors the imperfection of God.

9. Language, doctrine and written revelation are ultimately inadequate and meaningless. They are a barrier to the experience of enlightenment and truth.

10. An endless and confusing stream of "god-men," gurus and avatars impart enlightenment, but are limited in power and duration.

Biblical World View

1. God is eternally transcendent, "other" than creation (although he is immanent or omnipresent—Acts 17:28). Creatures are individual and unique (Col 1:16-17; 1 Cor 4:7; Is 55:8-9; 48:11).

2. God is a personality or Infinite Person. He is holy, to be worshiped (Rev 4:11). The Holy Spirit is a Person (Jn 16:13-14).

3. Humanity is fallen and sinful, although created in the image of God and therefore having great value. Moral evil is a reality. Satan is a personal, wicked entity, with his will set against God (Jer 17:5-9; Is 64:6; Rom 3:23; Jn 3:19; 8:44).

4. Existence of evil necessitates God's action. Forgiveness is offered via the death of Christ to atone for sin (Jn 3:16; Rom 5:8).

5. View of history and individual lives is linear. Problem of evil and suffering is permanently resolved by Christ's redemption, with the creation of a New Heaven and a New Earth (Rev 21:1-4; Heb 7:25-28; 9:12, 25-28). "Once for all."

6. Cosmology—Physical world is real and good (although fallen); it is not to be discounted. It has ramifications for spirituality and is to be integrated with spiritual reality (Gen 1:31).

7. Grace, atonement, and forgiveness are free (Eph 2:8-9). We are saved by the mercy and initiative of God.

8. God's perfection is not affected by the imperfection of the world, although he is moved to compassion (Jas 1:17; Jn 11:35).

9. Human language is rooted in reality. The Bible is valid and adequate to transmit God's message to humanity. Hence, we see Jesus as "the Word made flesh" (Jn 1:1-4).

10. Jesus of Nazareth is the unique, one-time incarnation of God (Heb 9:25-28). He does not have to "offer himself repeatedly."

Figure 1. Adapted from my original and used by permission of Spiritual Counterfeits Project, Inc.,© 1980, P.O. Box 2418, Berkeley, CA 94702.

spiritual evolution whereby we merely slide into another realm or move grudgingly on into a new body. If reincarnation were true, we would all be at the mercy of an imperfect and compulsive Deity for eternity, and nihilism would be the truest and most consistent philosophy.

Jesus of Nazareth came and died to stop "the wheel of birth, death and suffering," not to keep it rolling. If this is the qualification for the savior of the human race, then there can be only One.

> For you shall go out in joy,
>   and be led forth in peace;
> the mountains and the hills before you
>   shall break forth into singing,
>   and all the trees of the field shall clap their hands.
> Instead of the thorn shall come up the cypress;
>   instead of the brier shall come up the myrtle;
> and it shall be to the LORD for a memorial,
>   for an everlasting sign which shall not be cut off.
> (Is 55:12-13)

And I heard a loud voice from the throne saying, "Behold, the dwelling of God is with men. He will dwell with them, and they shall be his people, and God himself will be with them; he will wipe away every tear from their eyes, and death shall be no more, neither shall there be mourning nor crying nor pain any more, for the former things have passed away." (Rev 21:3-4)

Notes

Preface
[1]George Gallup, *Adventures in Immortality* (New York: McGraw Hill, 1982), pp. 137-38.
[2]Ibid.

Chapter 1: Reincarnation East and West
[1]*San Francisco Examiner*, 8 December 1977.
[2]The breakdown: Austria 20%; Canada 26%; France 23%; Britain 18%; Sweden 12%; U.S. 20%; West Germany 25%.
[3]Carl F. H. Henry, *God, Revelation and Authority*, 4 vols. (Waco, Tex.: Word Books, 1979), 4:610.
[4]Leoline L. Wright, *Reincarnation* (San Diego, Calif.: Point Loma Publications, 1975), p. 25.
[5]Joy Mills, Foreword in Virginia Hanson, ed., *Karma, The Universal Law of Harmony* (Wheaton, Ill.: Theosophical Publ. House, 1975).
[6]Quoted in *Who Is This Man and What Does He Want?* (Berkeley, Calif.: Spiritual Counterfeits Project, 1976), p. 1.
[7]Helen Wambach, lecture in Palo Alto, Calif., 15 July 1979 (my notes).
[8]Michael Paternoster, "Reincarnation—a Christian Critique," *Christian Parapsychologist*, September 1979, p. 124.

Chapter 2: Reincarnation and Karma
[1]Anna K. Winner, *The Basic Ideas of Occult Wisdom* (Wheaton, Ill.: Theosophical Publ. House, n.d.), p. 57.
[2]H. Spencer Lewis, *Mansions of the Soul* (San Jose, Calif.: Rosicrucian Library, 1930), p. 199.

[3]Interview in *Playboy* magazine, May 1981, p. 94.

[4]Helena Petrovna Blavatsky, "Karma—the Womb of Time," *The Theosophist*, vol. 5, no. 9 (Adyar, India, June 1884), p. 223.

[5]Quoted in Hanson, *Karma*, pp. 2, 27, 2.

[6]Some traditions speak of "the lords of karma" or the *Lipika*, as some Hindus call the "spiritual judge and jury." However, this notion seems to be held by a distinct minority, and most reincarnationists opt for the impersonal view, more on the order of Newton's law or the computer analogy.

[7]Quoted in Hanson, *Karma*, pp. 27, 32.

[8]Helena Petrovna Blavatsky, *The Secret Doctrine*, 2 vols. (Pasadena, Calif.: Theosophical Univ. Press, 1977), 2:420.

[9]Gnosticism is often thought of as a particular religion, namely, the Hellenistic Gnosticism that flourished in the second and third centuries and which was was one of the principal heresies that confronted the early church. In this book, *gnostic* and *gnosticism* will be employed as generic terms as defined in the text and applied to the philosophy that undergirds reincarnation.

[10]Adapted from Brooks Alexander, "Occult Philosophy and Mystical Experience," (Berkeley, Calif.: Spiritual Counterfeits Project, 1975), one of the best short explanations of this world view. (Many Buddhists would say that "All is suffering"—the fundamental tenet of Buddhism—and balk at the idea of union with God or the universe, since the existence of God is inconsequential in much of Buddhism, and the goal is to cease suffering by the attainment of non-existence.)

Chapter 3: A Short History of Reincarnation Teachings

[1]James H. Breasted, *Development of Religion and Thought in Ancient Egypt* (London: Hodder and Stoughton, 1912), p. 277.

[2]Swami Agehananda Bharati to author, 10 March 1981, Aarhus, Denmark.

[3]R. C. Zaehner, *Hinduism* (London: Oxford Univ. Press, 1962), pp. 75, 77.

[4]Quoted in Joseph Head and S. L. Cranston, eds., *Reincarnation: The Phoenix Fire Mystery* (New York: Warner Books, 1977), p. 61.

[5]W. Bryher, *Ruan* (New York: Pantheon, 1960), pp. 8-9.

[6]*Occult* is usually taken to mean black magic and the like, but the Latin root of the word means "hidden" or "secret," an allusion to the esoteric "deeper" truths supposedly known only to the enlightened elite. Many small movements of esoteric Christianity arose in the second millennium A.D. under the rubric of Gnosticism.

[7]C. S. Lewis, *Miracles* (New York: Macmillan Co., 1947), pp. 82-83.

Chapter 4: Reincarnation in the Bible and the Early Church

[1]Ronald A. Ward, "James," ed. D. Guthrie, J. A. Motyer, A. M. Stibbs, O. J. Wiseman, *The New Bible Commentary: Revised* (Grand Rapids: Eerdmans, 1970), p. 1230.

[2]Geddes MacGregor, *Reincarnation in Christianity* (Wheaton, Ill.: Quest Books, 1978), p. 16.

[3]Ibid., p. 42.

[4]Among the biblical passages which implicitly deny reincarnation are the following: 2 Sam 12:23; 14:14; Ps 78:39; Lk 23:39-43; Acts 17:31; 2 Cor 5:1, 4, 8;

6:2; Gal 2:16; 3:10-13; Eph 2:8-9; Phil 1:23; Heb 9:27; 10:12-14 and Rev 20: 11-15.

[5]Head and Cranston, *Phoenix Fire Mystery*, p. 134.

[6]Irenaeus' list (ca. 190) attests to the widespread acceptance of the New Testament canon by the end of the second century. His list was almost identical to our present canon.

[7]C. C. Richardson, ed., *Early Christian Fathers* (New York: Macmillan, 1970), pp. 371-72.

[8]Winner, *Basic Ideas*, p. 56.

[9]Wright, *Reincarnation*, p. 67.

[10]Kenneth Scott Latourette, *A History of Christianity* (New York: Harper & Row, 1953), p. 24.

[11]*Reincarnation and Christianity* (London: Wm. Rider and Son, 1909), p. 51.

[12]Justin Martyr, *Dialogue with Trypho*, trans. Thomas Falls (New York: Christian Heritage Press, 1948), p. 155.

[13]Head and Cranston, *Phoenix Fire Mystery*, p. 145.

[14]Allan Menzies, ed., *The Ante-Nicene Fathers*, vol. 10 (Grand Rapids: Eerdmans, 1978), pp. 474-75.

[15]Ibid., p. 447.

[16]David Christie-Murray, *Reincarnation: Ancient Beliefs and Modern Evidence* (London: David and Charles, 1981), p. 59.

[17]Philip Schaff, ed., *Nicene and Ante-Nicene Fathers of the Christian Church*, vol. 4 (Grand Rapids: Eerdmans, 1978), p. 209.

[18]Schaff and Wace, ed., *Nicene and Post-Nicene Fathers of the Christian Church*, vol. 5 (Grand Rapids: Eerdmans, 1979), p. 419.

[19]Ibid., p. 283.

[20]MacGregor, *Reincarnation in Christianity*, p. 91.

[21]Ibid., p. 94.

Chapter 5: Past-Life Recall

[1]Quoted in Head and Cranston, *The Phoenix Fire Mystery*, pp. 396-98.

[2]"Where Were You in 1643?" *Time*, 3 October 1977, p. 53.

[3]Public relations pamphlet from Valley of the Sun, Malibu, Calif., p. 3.

[4]NBC TV, "In Search of Reincarnation," aired in San Francisco, 8 April 1978.

[5]*Houston Chronicle*, 27 November 1977.

[6]ABC presentation on psychic phenomena, aired in San Francisco, 5 December 1978.

[7]*Contra Costa* (Calif.) *Times*, 2 September 1977.

[8]Helen Wambach, *Reliving Past Lives: The Evidence under Hypnosis* (New York: Harper & Row, 1978), p. 52.

[9]Lecture in Palo Alto, Calif., 15 July 1979.

[10]*Houston Chronicle*, 27 November 1977.

[11]Wambach, *Reliving Past Lives*, p. 151.

[12]*San Francisco Chronicle*, 10 March 1978, p. 24.

[13]Ian Stevenson, *Twenty Cases Suggestive of Reincarnation* (Charlottesville, Va.: Univ. Press of Virginia, 1966), p. 13.

[14]*Indianapolis Star*, 10 December 1978.

[15]One curious and revealing statement appears in the acknowledgments of Stevenson's book: "For early financial assistance and much encouragement, I am grateful to Mrs. Eileen J. Garrett, President, Parapsychology Foundation." Mrs. Garrett is considered by many to have been the most authentic and influential medium in Britain in recent times.

[16]Stevenson, *Twenty Cases,* pp. 2, 42.

[17]Ibid., p. 4.

[18]Ibid., p. 5.

[19]"Have You Lived Before?" *Family Circle,* 14 June 1978, p. 39.

[20]Harold I. Lief, "Commentary on Dr. Ian Stevenson's 'The Evidence of Man's Survival after Death,' " *Journal of Nervous and Mental Disease,* September 1977.

[21]Paternoster, "Reincarnation—A Christian Critique," p. 136.

[22]Ibid., p. 137.

[23]Harold Rosen, *A Scientific Report on "The Search for Bridey Murphy"* (New York: Julian, 1956), p. 54.

[24]Joseph Crehan, *Christian Parapsychologist,* March 1980, p. 56.

[25]MacGregor, *Reincarnation in Christianity,* p. 118.

[26]Stevenson, *Twenty Cases,* p. 3.

[27]Quoted in Head and Cranston, *Phoenix Fire Mystery,* p. 429.

[28]Stevenson, *Twenty Cases,* p. 246.

[29]"Have You Lived Before?" p. 39.

[30]"Where Were You in 1643?" p. 53.

[31]*Long Beach Independent-Press Telegram,* 6 June 1980.

Chapter 6: Sorting It Out: Possible Explanations of Past-Life Recall

[1]Wambach, *Reliving Past Lives,* pp. 14, 41.

[2]Chris Westphal, "There May Be Reincarnation," *Contra Costa Times,* 2 September 1977.

[3]Wambach, *Reliving Past Lives,* pp. 87, 85.

[4]Quoted in Paternoster, "Reincarnation—A Christian Critique," p. 136.

[5]*San Francisco Examiner,* 17 March 1977, p. 24.

[6]"Where Were You in 1643?" p. 53.

[7]Henry Gris, "Robert Cummings Tells of His Next Life 100 Years from Now," *National Enquirer,* 11 September 1979, p. 26.

[8]Stevenson, *Twenty Cases,* p. 313.

[9]Ibid., p. 317.

[10]Ibid., p. 351.

[11]*Long Beach Independent-Press Telegram,* 6 June 1980, p. A-24.

[12]Wambach, *Reliving Past Lives,* pp. 41-42.

[13]Jess Stearn, "Could She Possibly Have Known Jesus?" *Ladies Home Journal,* October 1972, p. 88.

[14]Ibid.

[15]Stevenson, *Twenty Cases,* p. 48.

[16]Ibid., p. 345.

[17]Paul Twitchell, *The Eck Satsang Discourses,* 1st series, no. 3 (Las Vegas: Eckankar, 1970-71), p. 2.

[18]Edmond Gruss, *What about the Ouija Board?* (Chicago: Moody Press, 1973), p. 16.

[19]Quoted in Stevenson, *Twenty Cases,* p. 340.

[20]Ibid., p. 321.

[21]John Keel, *UFO's: Operation Trojan Horse* (New York: G. P. Putnam's Sons, 1970), p. 122.

[22]*Knoxville News-Sentinel,* 22 August 1979.

[23]Morton Kelsey, *Afterlife* (New York: Paulist Press, 1979), p. 233.

Chapter 7: World Views in Conflict: The Arguments for and against Reincarnation

[1]S. L. Cranston in a letter to the editor, *Christian Parapsychologist,* June 1980.

[2]Sri Chinmoy, *The Movement Newspaper* (Los Angeles), March 1980, p. 1.

[3]MacGregor, *Reincarnation in Christianity,* p. 116.

[4]Henry, *God, Revelation and Authority,* 4:614.

[5]MacGregor, *Reincarnation in Christianity,* p. 165.

[6]Paternoster, "Reincarnation—A Christian Critique," p. 127.

[7]Morris, quoted in J. I. Packer, *Knowing God* (Downers Grove, Ill.: InterVarsity Press, 1973), p. 130.

[8]Two other passages which elaborate on Christian judgment are John 9:39-41 and Romans 2:1-16.

[9]H. O. Wiley, *Christian Theology* (Kansas City, Mo.: Beacon Hill Press, 1940), pp. 445-46.

[10]*The Upanishads, Breath of the Eternal,* trans. Swami Prabhavananda and Frederick Manchester (New York: Pantheon Books, 1957), p. 56.

[11]John Wenham, *The Goodness of God* (Downers Grove, Ill.: InterVarsity Press, 1974), p. 184.

[12]Tim Dailey, *Reincarnation and Christianity* (Milwaukee: CARIS, 1975), p. 4.

[13]Quoted in Head and Cranston, *Phoenix Fire Mystery,* p. 54.

Chapter 8: Philosophical and Moral Objections to Reincarnation

[1]Helena Petrovna Blavatsky, *The Key to Theosophy* (New York: Theosophical Publ. House, 1889), pp. 46-47.

[2]Head and Cranston, *Phoenix Fire Mystery,* p. 13.

[3]There is a notable dichotomy between the bare bones of Hindu-Buddhist philosophy and the way people actually live it out. Even gurus and Buddhist holy men hope—although the hope is for samadhi, nirvana or a better lot in the next life. They rarely if ever acknowledge the eternal cyclic despair that lies behind their beliefs.

[4]Edward Ryall, *Born Twice–Total Recall of a Seventeenth Century Life* (New York: Harper & Row, 1974), p. 3.

[5]John Weldon, "Reincarnation: A Billion People's View of Reality" (manuscript prepared for Spiritual Counterfeits Project, Berkeley, 1979).

[6]Henry, *God, Revelation and Authority,* 4:71.

[7]MacGregor, *Reincarnation in Christianity,* pp. 74-75.

[8]*The Thirteen Principal Upanishads* (London: Oxford Univ. Press, 1921), Maitri Upanishad 3:4.

[9]MacGregor, *Reincarnation in Christianity,* p. 73.

[10]Arthur Robson, "Infinite Continuity in Multimillionfold Diversity," in Hanson,

Karma, p. 65.

[11] Wright, *Reincarnation*, p. 21.

[12] Ibid., p. 7.

[13] Blavatsky, "Original Programme," in *Collected Writings*, vol. 3 (Ostende, Belgium, 1886), p. 170.

[14] Walter Martin, *The Riddle of Reincarnation* (Santa Ana, Calif.: Vision House, 1977), p. 26.

[15] Paternoster, "Reincarnation—A Christian Critique," p. 126.

[16] Quoted in Head and Cranston, *Phoenix Fire Mystery*, p. 231.

[17] *The Upanishads*, p. 118.

[18] Zaehner, *Hinduism*, p. 86.

[19] Quoted in Head and Cranston, *Phoenix Fire Mystery*, p. 231.

[20] *Long Beach Independent-Press Telegram*, 6 June 1980.

[21] *The Movement Newspaper*, August 1980, pp. 22-23.

Chapter 9: Theological Objections

[1] *The Writings of Irenaeus*, vol 1 (Edinburgh: T. T. Clark, 1868), p. 2.

[2] Clarence R. Pedersen, "The Source of Becauses," in Hanson, *Karma*, p. 36.

[3] Ibid., p. 37.

[4] Quoted in C. J. Ducasse, *The Belief in a Life after Death* (Springfield, Ill.: C. C. Thomas, 1961), p. 209.

[5] Blavatsky, *Key to Theosophy*, p. 135.

[6] Ibid., p. 27.

[7] Quoted in Head and Cranston, *Phoenix Fire Mystery*, p. 59.

[8] MacGregor, *Reincarnation in Christianity*, p. 24.

[9] Lecture in Palo Alto, Calif., 15 July 1979.

[10] Harry Blamires, *The Christian Mind* (Ann Arbor: Servant Books, 1978), p. 89.

Chapter 10: Theological Hybrids

[1] Not all mysticism should be rejected offhand; in its classical sense, mysticism may be defined as the seeking of the experience of the presence of God, or union with God and his will. Needless to say, these concepts are quite biblical. So, in that sense we may say that God calls all believers to be mystics. Christianity has a rich heritage of orthodox mysticism and pietism, which has often (e.g., in the Middle Ages) been a bulwark of the church.

[2] MacGregor, *Reincarnation in Christianity*, p. 123.

[3] Paternoster, "Reincarnation—A Christian Critique," p. 126.

[4] Quoted in Head and Cranston, *Phoenix Fire Mystery*, pp. 504-45.

[5] Friedrich Gogarten, *Die Religiose Entscheidung*, quoted in MacGregor, *Reincarnation in Christianity*, p. 148.

Subject Index

Index of Biblical Texts